TOTEM TALES OF OLD SEATTLE

is the gaudy, primitive and hilarious collection of tales, legends and anecdotes that brings to life a willful, fun-loving frontier—and a city that's never been tamed.

"This is a rollicking tale that makes you regret you weren't around to see the actual happenings of a hundred years ago. Today, however, nothing could be more fun than Gordon Newell's approach to what might be called, in the broad sense, 'history.' In addition to the tremendous amount of material, there is probably the most wondrous humor one could find!"

TOTEM TALES OF OLD SEATTLE

Legends and Anecdotes
By
GORDON NEWELL
AND TOTEMIZER
DON SHERWOOD

A COMSTOCK EDITION

BALLANTINE BOOKS — NEW YORK

SBN 345-24141-X-150

This edition published by arrangement with
Superior Publishing Company

First Printing: August 1974

Printed in the United States of America

Cover photo by Art Holt

A Comstock Edition

BALLANTINE BOOKS
A Division of Random House, Inc.
201 East 50th Street, New York, N.Y. 10022

Simultaneously published by
Ballantine Books, Ltd., Toronto, Canada

FOREWORD

ON READING TOTEM POLES AND WRITING HISTORY

Totem poles are the theme of this book about Old Seattle, a choice which was made for a number of reasons. In the first place, they seem to symbolize the colorful Northwest Frontier city that was Old Seattle. It's true that the really expert totem-makers lived a bit further north, along the British Columbia and Alaska coast, but the amiable Puget Sound Indians who used to picnic along the shore of Elliott Bay did a little carving of their own. They did it the way they did almost everything . . . in a lazy, easy-going sort of way like old Henry Yesler whittling a white pine stick on his front porch in the summer time. Since they didn't amount to much anyway, it was sometimes easier to throw last summer's totems on the fire than to go down to the beach in the winter rain for driftwood.

Most of Seattle's present-day totem poles are imports from Up North, but that doesn't alter the fact that Seattle and totem poles just naturally go together, like steamed clams and melted butter.

Totem poles seemed especially fitting for this book, too, because they present the Indian's version of history, which was highly informal and well laced with legend. That's the kind of history this is, although some scholarly and well-meaning critics will probably deny that it's any kind of history at all. In a way, perhaps, it isn't. History is something that you have to be able to prove in black and white. Legends are more fun; they don't have to be probed and certified, and in many ways, I think, they do a better job of bringing the past back to vivid life than does history itself.

It can't be proven that Doc Maynard saluted the infant city of Seattle with a square-faced whiskey bottle, that a Skid Road Socialist put Teddy Roosevelt in his place, or that World War I welders sealed their unpopular foreman up in the skin of the ship they were building, but surely such legends are as much a part of the fabric of Old Seattle as any cold facts in the archives of the city. They are much a part of this book, and for them I make no apology.

The third, and probably the most important reason for the totemic tone of this book is Don Sherwood, who drew the unique illustrations for it. Actually, this book tells its story twice; once in the text and again in Don Sherwood's totem poles. The cartoon totems are a bit different from the ones the Indians carved in wood, but basically they do the same job of telling a story in pictures rather than in words. Like real Indian totems, the Sherwood drawings may be confusing unless you have the key, and in this case the key to the totem is the chapter it illustrates. After reading the chapter it will be found that the accompanying totem comes into focus to tell its perfectly logical, if sometimes hilarious, story. For readers who like to check the answers to the puzzles they've solved, there's an answer sheet in the back of the book.

Another thing about Don Sherwood's totems is worth mentioning. It may take an expert or a historian to appreciate it, but the details of each intricate drawing are entirely authentic, if somewhat exaggerated. Hours of research went into the assurance that everything from the glue pot that started the Great Fire to the corncob pipe of Mayor Hi Gill is drawn as it really was. This quality makes them somewhat easier to decipher than, say, the famous Pioneer Place Totem.

Of course even that becomes simplified with the knowledge that the top figure is a raven and that the top man on the totem pole usually identified the clan whose legendary history it tells; that the object in Raven's beak is the moon. It's fairly obvious that the blushing lady below is of the Raven Clan and that she has either married or been carrying on with a Frog Clansman.[1] Admittedly, things get more complicated when we work down to Mink (Even Don Sherwood doesn't know how *he* got in the act) and his Raven pal, who went for a cruise in Killer Whale, an oily experience which turned Mink brown from rolling in rotten wood to clean himself.

---

[1] . . . And still is, as you'll notice if you look closely.

The ubiquitous Frog clan is also represented on another famous Seattle totem—the one at Belvedere Place in West Seattle, whose likeness adorns the cover of the city telephone directory. Here, however, the gnawing, flat-tailed figure at the top shows that this is primarily the story of the Beaver Clan, who were mighty fishermen and killers of whales despite the weakening influence of the bothersome Frogs.

There are other interesting totems in Seattle and its vicinity, some old, like the one at Belvedere Place, some replicas of old ones, and some new, for totem carving is not a lost art. Indians like Joseph Hillaire of the Lummis and Chief William Shelton, who carved the tall totem which stands on the state capitol grounds in Olympia, have adapted their ancient trade to modern tools. And white men have learned the totemic art, too. The sweeping lines of the modern poles at Northgate Shopping Center and in the Bon Marche are the work of Dudley Carter, a Seattle sculptor who is quite un-Indianlike in everything but his handling of axe and adze. Yes, totems are a part of Seattle's personality and it is right that they should help to tell the story of Seattle which, as in any great city, is part history and part legend . . . and partly a blending of the two.

A Seattle industry, the Skyway Luggage Company, distributes replicas of the Pioneer Place Totem Pole to friends and customers to attract attention to the firm and to the city. The firm's head, Henry L. Kotkins, says, "I've found that people all over the world are fascinated by totem poles. I feel that totem poles reflect the personality of this area".

And that just about sums up the purpose of this book . . . to reflect the personality of a city with a fabulous past; to neither lampoon it or treat it with undue gravity, but to tell, a little in the manner of the Totem Tales of the Northwest Indians, the gaudy, primitive, laughing story of a frontier town that has never been entirely tamed . . . the story of Old Seattle.

GORDON NEWELL
Seattle, Washington
April 1, 1956

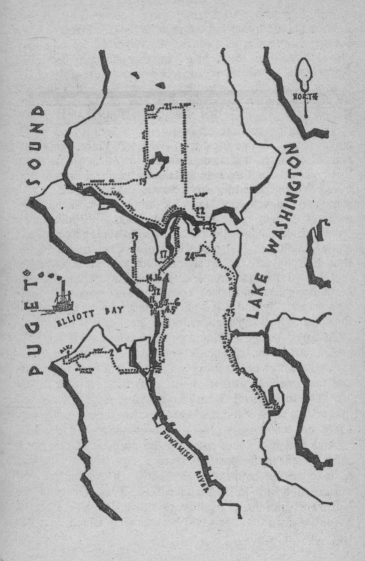

OLD SEATTLE

By Carlton Fitchett

How we loved the old Seattle,
In the days so brave and fine,
And the street cars' merry rattle
On the Yesler Cable Line.

And the gold rush to Alaska,
Men with shovels, picks and pans;
And the battleship Nebraska,
On the keel-blocks at Moran's.

When the twilight breeze was straying,
Jam-packed street cars we would take
Out to hear Dad Wagner playing
Summer concerts at the Lake.

Or with throngs of other merry
Girls and fellows we'd embark
On the West Seattle ferry
For a fling at Luna Park.

How we thrilled to watch them sluicing
Down the crown of Denny Hill,
While Mark Matthews was unloosing
Verbal blasts at Hiram Gill.

How we flocked to pay admission
When the A-Y-P began,
Just to see the exposition
And the hubba-hubba man.

Yes, we love those days so splendid,
Full of unexpected treats,
When the Indian women vended
Butter clams on downtown streets.

FROM THE SEATTLE POST-INTELLIGENCER

THE TOTEM POLE
PIONEER PLACE

The original Pioneer Place Totem Pole was brought to Seattle in 1899 by an Alaskan excursion party jointly sponsored by the Seattle Chamber of Commerce and the Post Intelligencer. Carved by the Tlingit Tribe on Tongass Island of Southeast Alaska, the pole was already at least fifty years old at the time of its arrival in Seattle. The orignal pole was burned by vandals in 1938 and was replaced by the present totem which is an almost exact replica, carved by later Alaska Indians.

The pole's figures, from top to bottom, are as follows:

RAVEN: (culture Hero) at the head of the totem indicates the family lineage. Holds the MOON in his mouth.

WOMAN: Holding her FROG CHILD.

FROG: Husband of the woman.

MINK.

RAVEN.

KILLER WHALE: Blow-hole carved to represent a face, a seal in its mouth.

RAVEN-AT-THE-HEAD-OF-NASS: Grandfather of Raven.

Three myths are symbolized on this Totem Pole. The symbols are standardized, but each lineage has its own version of the myths.

1. Raven, through trickery, gets himself born as a child and is adopted by Raven-At-The-Head-Of-Nass, from whom he steals the sun and moon, which the old grandfather had been keeping in his lodge. Raven throws the sun and moon into the sky, after which he makes his escape through the smoke hole, thus becoming a black bird.

2. Many intermarriages between members of Raven Clan transformed into human form (Woman in this instance) and Frogs, who have also taken on human forms, result in complications when children arrive in original frog form.

3. Mink and Raven take a sea voyage in the belly of Killer Whale, feasting until they come to the whale's heart. When they carve out that vital organ Whale dies and they are washed ashore. They finish off the carcass on the beach, but find that their adventure has left Raven sleek and oily while Mink has become dirty-brown from rolling in rotten wood in order to clean himself.

TOTEM TALES
OF OLD SEATTLE

THE LANDING OF THE PILGRIMS

FISH! said young Arthur Denny explosively. "Lord love a herrin', Mary, aint you had enough fish, comin' down the river in that gurry-barge of Chenweth's?"

Mary Denny looked primly pretty for all the rash of bumpy Williamette River mosquito bites that peppered her nose and forehead, for the stay at Portland had been long enough to remove the stains of four months on the Oregon Trail.

"No need to blaspheme Arthur", she told her husband severely. "Fish is good, nourishing food and he's offering us the whole big salmon for just one bit". She nodded solemnly toward the grinning, flat-headed Chinook brave who held a shining King Salmon enticingly in both grimy paws as his canoe rubbed its cedar sides against the schooner's quarter.

Denny's gray-blue eyes swept the cramped deck of the 73-foot *Exact*. The little knot of women, who had been tethering children to the foremast, was moving toward them, obviously attracted by the salmon salesman in the canoe alongside. Arthur Denny wasn't much more than old enough to vote, but leadership of the wagon train that had brought them from Cherry Grove, Illinois, to the Oregon Country had given him a wisdom beyond his years. A surprisingly warm smile softened the lines of his long, serious

1

face. "Take it quick, Mary", he chuckled. "Those other female pilgrims up for'ard've smelled a bargain, which aint surprisin', considerin' what it is. There's no stoppin' you now and you might as well get that twenty-pounder your friend's nursin' so loving-like. Can't deny it's a powerful lot of fish for ten cents".

Mary Denny's quick smile answered her husband. "Here, take Louise and Lenora[1] up forward with the other children while I get the money out of my reticule. Mrs. Alexander's almost here and she's not one to turn down a bargain".

The two little girls clung to their mother's skirt in silent protest. "We don't *wike* to be tied up wike puppy-dogs", four-year-old Lenora announced solemnly, but when their tall father held out his hands to them they went with him. Even the grown-up people did what their daddy told them to do, especially when they were traveling through Indian country.

"Can't say I blame you," their father admitted. He was remembering the last leg of the long, long journey from Knox County, Illinois, to the mouth of the Columbia River; the voyage downstream from the Cascades of the Columbia to Portland in Judge Chenoweth's ancient brig *Henry,* too far gone in senile decay to sail the ocean and reduced to hauling salted fish on the river. The adults of the party, bone-tired from the trek across the continent, had tried to sleep on blankets spread across the tops of fish barrels in the hold. The children. . . half the party were children . . . played on deck in the watery river sunlight, tied to the masts, as Lenora had said, like puppy-dogs. There had been no bulwarks on the disreputable *Henry* and the mothers had been too tired to keep close watch on the children. The ravening mosquitoes and the fish-stinking bilge of the old hulk had robbed both sleep and play of any real pleasure.

Captain Folger's schooner *Exact* was a different propo-

---

[1] Margaret Lenora Denny, who survived the perils of the Overland Trail as a child of four, died in an automobile accident on the Seattle-Tacoma Highway at the age of 67.

sition entirely; a trim, taut Nantucket craft with neatly sanded decks and a snug cabin lined with comfortable bunks. Of course things weren't all beer and skittles. An ocean voyage up the coast of Oregon in a 70-ton schooner full of kids and women; a November voyage to a strange place called Puget's Sound. And the two-month-old baby, Rolland, puny and ailing and probably crying fretfully in the cabin below. The cow's milk they'd been able to get for him in Portland seemed to have done him good, but there'd be no cows where they were going, and the Lord only knew whether tiny, pinch-faced Rolland would live to get there anyway.

Up forward twenty-one-year-old Charley Terry was just turning from the open hold, wiping the sweat of concentration and worry from his swarthy forehead. The gesture left dirty smudges, almost as black as his thick hair and young man's beard, but the smudges didn't detract from his look of eager determination. Charley was the devil-may-care bachelor of the party, darkly handsome, with the deep-set, shining eyes of a visionary. But Charley was equipped with the hard common-sense of a New England trader. That last keg of brandy, just swayed into the hold under the hopeful eyes of a crowd of bearded miners, would be part of the stock for the first store in the new city they were going to build on Puget's Sound. Arthur Denny didn't hold with drunkenness, but city-builders had to be practical. Folks aren't going to do their trading in a town where a man can't have a drink and a bit of a fling if he's a mind to.

Back aft Captain Folger had been lounging, loose-jointed as a yankee toy at the schooner's tiller, but he wasn't missing anything. "Ef'n yer goods'r all aboard, Mr. Terry", he called nasally through cupped hands, "and if the ladies'll be good enough t'remove that flotilla of young'uns from my mainmast, I'll set about gettin' under way. Tide'll be ebbin' shortly and I've seen the bar look a sight worse'n it does now".

On the tiny quarterdeck there was a bustle of movement as the women completed their bargaining with the Indian fishermen. A half dozen big salmon lay on the deck when the Chinook, still grinning happily, swung his light canoe away from the ship. It was, as Arthur Denny had observed, a lot of fish for ten cents.

The cabin suddenly seemed stuffy and crowded when everyone was in it . . . men, women, children and fish, all shooed below while the *Exact's* crew prepared to work her across the river bar and safely out to sea. Habit was strong in Arthur Denny and he mentally called the roll, as he had done each evening on the overland trail: his brother-in-law, Carson Boren looked pinched and unhappy, sitting hunched up on a low bunk with his women-folk on either side of him—his pretty dark-eyed wife, Mary and his even prettier sister, Louisa. Mary looked apprehensive, like her husband. Both of them had been seasick on the *Henry,* the old brig that only sailed the inland river. Louisa looked bright and glowing and Denny thought he knew why. His kid brother, Dave, and Louisa Boren had acted mighty prim and proper all the way out to Oregon, but they weren't fooling him much. He figured they were sweet on each other, and Dave was up on Puget's Sound getting things ready for the folks coming on the *Exact.*

The old man of the party, thirty-four-year-old Bill Bell, big and amiable as a Saint Bernard . . . and almost as shaggy in his frontier whiskers and uncut hair, was sharpening a stag-handled knife on the sole of one boot. Mrs. Bell was poking at the wood fire in the smoky little iron stove that was anchored down in the center of the cabin. It was obvious that they were hankering for a fresh salmon breakfast. The salmon were all jumbled together in a keg beside the stove and the warmth was getting to them. That probably helped to explain the pained looks of Cars Boren and his wife. No doubt about it, it *was* getting close and fragrant in the cabin of the *Exact.*

John Low was up on deck. Captain Folger was depending on him to pilot the schooner to their unnamed new town on Puget's Sound. That gave him the privileges of the quarterdeck while the ship was getting under way. Anyway, John was getting to be an old man like Bill Bell and a cabin-full of noisy kids was likely to get on his nerves. John Low was a good thirty years old, if he was a day.

Mrs. Low and Mrs. Alexander were busy stowing kids and baggage in and under and around the crowded bunks. Mrs. Alexander was bossing the job, of course. She wasn't really one of the party. She and her husband were headed for Olympia, which was already a settled town with a name and a postoffice. Arthur Denny suspected that Mrs. Alexander took a sort of patronizing attitude toward them on that account. Not that she wasn't helpful and pleasant enough. She was just a mite too pleased with herself and the civilized future she had planned for herself to please young Denny. He hoped she'd be seasick, but he was afraid she wouldn't be. She seemed far too competent and superior for seasickness.

The schooner was swooping to the first Pacific ocean rollers when Bill Bell had his knife properly sharpened and Mrs. Bell's salmon properly barbecued. The hot grease was hissing back and forth in the pan and something that must have been bilge water was gurgling under the cabin floor boards. Cars Boren's long nose had a greenish tinge around the nostrils and he was holding his head in both hands. Arthur Denny couldn't decide which smelled the worst, the hot grease or the disturbed bilge water.

Up on deck the miners were singing and swigging from bottles which they passed from hand to hand. They were playing poker on the hatch cover and they seemed to be having a wonderful time. The dashing bachelor, Charley Terry was singing and playing cards with them and, Denny suspected, swigging from the bottles with them, too. The miners were headed for the Queen Charlotte Islands, looking for gold, and they weren't burdened with wives or sick kids or kegs of slimy fish.

A dash of icy spray rattled against the companionway overhead and the smell of hot grease and bilge swept over Denny like an ocean breaker. He started shakily toward the companionway ladder, but he didn't make it. Even as the nausea wracked him he felt shame that the others should witness his disgrace, but when he was able to turn and crawl toward his bunk he saw that almost all of them were busy being as superhumanly ill as he was: all except that infuriating Mrs. Alexander. She was calmly steadying her frying pan with one hand and turning half-cooked salmon with the other.

After a while—it seemed like maybe a hundred years— Denny was able to turn his head from the creaking wall beside his bunk. He almost forgot his sickness then. Mrs. Alexander, the superior woman, was stretched full length upon the pitching deck, her right hand still grasping the pan of fish. He had never seen a sicker woman.

"Mrs. Alexander!", he called, "are you alive?"

The unfortunate woman could only flutter the hand not encumbered by the frying pan to indicate that she was, indeed, still living, even though not for long.

Afterward Denny admitted that it was a terrible thing to do, but he just couldn't help it. "Why don't you get up and finish cooking your fish, Mrs. Alexander, Ma'am", he called wanly. At the horrible word fish Mrs. Alexander was swept by a new wave of nausea. Thereafter, until weakness overcame him, Arthur Denny repeated his question at intervals: "Why are you lying there, ma'am? Why don't you get up and cook your fish?" And at each query Mrs. Alexander discovered new wells of violent illness. "I just didn't know I had it in me", she admitted afterward.

Afterward Charles Terry, warmed by companionship and rum, came down to get some cigars from his stock. He was planning to treat the jolly miners, but he never did. He succeeded in opening his trunk, but only in time to use it as he had never, never intended to.

And that made it one hundred percent.

John Low, the ancient of thirty-one, had been at sea before and he was above decks when the schooner rounded Cape Flattery and stood in toward Juan de Fuca Strait and Puget Sound. He it was, with the younger brothers of Denny and Terry, who had first scouted the site of the new city that was to be, and he was one of the very few people in the world who knew where it was. Captain Folger was counting on him to point it out and if he had stayed below with the others the schooner would probably have sailed right on past and delivered the pilgrims at Olympia. And the way they felt they would probably have stayed there.

There was the stuff of heroes in John Low. However sick and empty he might feel, he was on the quarterdeck to con the *Exact* on stage for the opening scene in the drama of a great city's birth. It was a watery, dreary stage setting, with the shining mountains hidden behind sopping clouds and the sombre firs whipping to the slash of wind and rain, but there were actors, props and an audience.

John Low had been there six weeks before, along with David Denny and Lee Terry. While Low returned to Portland to bring the rest of the party along, Denny and Terry stayed to begin the actual building of their city. It would rise, they decided, on the long, low point at the south entrance of the bay, a spot called Smaquamox by the Indians, but which looked so promising to them that they decided to name their city New York. The two teen-aged boys built a log cabin while Low was walking the two hundred miles back to Portland. They built it all but the roof, that is, for when they got that far they found that they had no tool for splitting cedar stakes. Terry set out for the Hudson's Bay post at Nisqually to buy a frow.[2]

The city was left with a population of one, a bearded man of nineteen huddled in wet blankets in a roofless cabin. Denny had cut his foot with an ax and could barely hobble around. He was burning with malarial fever too, and he had a thumping toothache. While he waited for the *Exact* he felt even worse than the other pilgrims in the little ship's cabin. At least they could enjoy the luxury of spurning good food. David Denny was half starved. A family of skunks had moved in with him in the city's only building. They had eaten all his food.

A party of Duwamish Indians were camped down by Duwamish Head. It was a fishing party, but business was always secondary to pleasure as far as they were concerned. When the *Exact* came drifting through the rain to anchor off the point the Indians dropped their nets and

---

[2] Terry made the trip with Luther Collins on his cattle scow. Collins, with Henry Van Asselt and Jacob Maple, had staked claims in the Duwamish River Valley in September. Afer a while their settlement became Georgetown.

hiked up the beach to see the excitement. David Denny hobbled down to the water's edge, draped in a wet blanket and with his aching jaws tied up in a rag. It was hard to pick him from the Indians, except that he looked more miserable than they did.

The pioneer women looked shoreward and what they saw was no beautiful vision; one roofless cabin between the dark, tremendous forest and the lonely beach. A scarecrow figure waving to them and naked Indians moving toward the landing place. And all made more depressing still by the steady, drumming fall of the cold November rain.

Mrs. Alexander had recovered pretty well from the salmon and the *Exact's* bilge and the effects of Arthur Denny's humor. She was going on south to the civilized town of Olympia, and she watched the drama of Seattle's founding from the schooner's deck . . . the women weeping in the crowded longboat and the tears being washed away by the unending rain. Mrs. Denny and Mrs. Boren and Mrs. Bell each carrying a baby in her arms, and Mrs. Low trying to comfort a two-year-old girl. Their possessions had been piled at the water's edge and the tide was coming in. The men were trying to rescue the boxes and chests before they were carried away by the sea or the curious Indians who didn't know that they were watching a great city being born.

Mrs. Alexander was sorry for them; even for Arthur Denny, who had made her even more miserable than necessary on the voyage up the coast. She was sorriest of all for Mrs. Denny. Her baby, Rolland, was only two months old and she was sick with malaria as well as the sea, and it was sad to see her going through the November rain to a city of one house, and that without a roof.

Rolland Denny, two months, was the youngest of the party. William Bell was the oldest. It was well that the pioneers had youth. They had little enough besides, or so it seemed to Mrs. Alexander, who was going on to a real city.

That's the way it looked at eight o'clock on the morning of November 13, 1851, at a place the Indians called Smaquamox and the Terry brothers called New York.

OLD MAN SEATTLE

THE INDIANS who strolled up the beach from Duwamish Head to Alki Point to watch a city being born were members of the Duwamish and Suquamish tribes.[1] They were amiable enough, but they probably depressed the founding fathers, who already had enough to contend with in the way of dripping skies, weeping wives and lack of suitable accommodations.

These Indians were undersized and very dirty. Their legs were bowed like those of Texas cowhands, but for a different reason. They spent most of their time squatting in narrow canoes and were just as averse to walking as the present day residents of their tribal picnic ground who spend much time driving around look for parking places.

The welcoming committee at Alki Point was dressed for the weather. Since countless generations of Duwamish and Suquamish had satisfied themselves that no garment known to man will keep out a real Puget Sound November rain they had long ago bowed to the inevitable. While they were out in it they wore practically nothing. That kept their clothes dry at home and it didn't bother them much, because they kept themselves coated from top to bottom with

---

[1] The Duwamish lived mostly on Lake Washington, the Suquamish on Puget Sound.

well aged dogfish oil. It bothered the pilgrims considerably, however; the sight of the delegation was bad enough, but the wonderful aroma of dogfish oil was the last straw for a group of people whose original nausea had been brought on by as harmless an odor as that of frying salmon. All in all, the welcome accorded the new arrivals from the *Exact* was a far cry from a band and Chamber of Commerce committee.

There were, of course, exceptions. even among the generally uninspiring aborigines who lived in the Elliott Bay area. Although it wasn't talked about in the better Duwamish and Suquamish circles, the exceptions were usually the result of frequent visits made by certain undesirable neighbors from up north. The Haidas of British Columbia were big and tough and handsome. They liked to take their summer vacations on Puget Sound, paying their expenses by grabbing everything in sight that seemed worth grabbing.

The Sound Indians had a single well-rehearsed tactic when the Haidas came a-raiding. They grabbed a few clams and took off at the highest possible speed for the tall timber. Sometimes an attractive squaw would pause for a second look at the broad-shouldered, straight-legged visitors . . . or would, perhaps, sprain her ankle while in maidenly flight. When that happened she, too, was inevitably grabbed.

The Chief of the Duwamish and Suquamish was an exception. The pioneers who knew him personally all agreed that he was an impressive looking man, although few of them agreed on the spelling of his name. *Sealth, See-Alt, Se-at-lee, Seattle.* You can find these and more in the old manuscripts. But this much is certain. He was six feet tall with all the massive dignity of a Roman senator, and when he was orating you could hear every word he said for half a mile against the wind. Seattle was quite a man.

He was born on Blake Island while the white men on the East Coast were busy fighting in a revolution against the English. He didn't know anything about white men until he was about six years old. That was in 1792, and to his dying day Seattle remembered the excitement in the island camp when the big canoe with the white wings came into the bay.

It was Captain George Vancouver with his first lieutenant, Peter Puget, on the *Discovery*. As far as white men were concerned neither Seattle nor his tribe nor the country they lived in had existed until that year.

Seattle's father was Schweabe, who was Chief of the Suquamish, or as nearly a chief as anyone in that indolent and loosely organized group of people. His mother, Scholitza, was tall and of queenly bearing, with the slight Oriental cast of features that hinted of Haida blood. By Suquamish standards young Seattle was a privileged child. Other people paddled his canoe for him, so he was able to stretch his legs and avoid the tribal deformity. His family had the pick of the tribal food, so he grew big and strong, and his head showed little sign of the tight binding that flattened the skulls of many of his contemporaries.

When the pilgrims landed at Alki, Seattle was about 65 years old, still tall, broad shouldered and deep chested, but leaning on a staff as befitted his age and dignity. His massive, lined face and shoulder length gray hair added to his look of a benign old philosopher. More important, he was genuinely friendly toward the white men. Almost all the solid citizens of the new town on Elliott Bay came to like and respect "Old Man Seattle". In the end they named their city for him. This they considered the ultimate in civic honor, although to poor old Seattle it was a curse that disturbed him a good deal more than a guilty conscience. His white friends thought he was just being modest when he begged them not to attach his name to their city, but he was serious. More than that, he was scared half to death. The Chief had become a good Christian in his old age,[2] but he hadn't been able to forget a lifetime of tribal doctrine. It was the firm belief of the Indians that the dead awaken from their slumber when their names are mentioned by the living. The white men claimed their town was going to become a great city which would be known all over the world.

---

[2] At his Christian baptism, Chief Seattle, a noted boatman in his own right, was named Noah—Noah Sealth.

Seattle had unpleasant visions of his name in daily use on thousands of tongues and of himself whirling like a top in his grave. It was a sobering reflection and Seattle no doubt felt as did the man who, being ridden out of town on a rail, observed that if it weren't for the honor of the thing he would just as soon have walked.

The kindly and dignified old chief was immortalized in spite of himself, and even the founding fathers who knew him never suspected that in his youth he was considered a dangerous hoodlum who barely escaped hanging for murder. Like many great men of all races, Seattle outlived his wild and wooly youth to achieve a respectable and dignified place in history.

Seattle's downfall was a shrewish wife. Being only human and a man, Seattle discovered that it was more pleasant spending evenings out with the boys than in a smoky cedar house listening to a sharp-tongued squaw. He took to gambling and it became a passion with him. While he gambled with the deer's bone dice he smoked kinnikinnick in his wooden pipe . . . the dried weed that inflamed his brain and made him feel even bigger and stronger than he was.

The smoking and the gambling didn't improve Seattle's temper. When he suspected a gambling companion of cheating he didn't waste time arguing about it. He beat the daylights out of him. Before long Seattle had a reputation as a very rough character who would just as soon whack you over the head with a madrona-wood war club as look at you.

Along about 1836 Seattle discovered a young Nisqually buck, whom he suspected of cheating at *slaha'lb,* hanging around the Hudson's Bay post on the upper sound. Seattle had visited the post to trade furs for a new musket, which he immediately ruined by using it to club the errant brave over the head.

Dr. Tolmie had Seattle thrown out of the post, observing in his journal that "an Indian of the So-quo-mish tribe, by name See alt," had created quite a disturbance around the place. He added, "At best this fellow is a scamp, and like

Steilacoom has a black heart. He is always ready to pick a quarrel".

The good doctor was even more disturbed when he learned that Seattle had purchased the British musket for the purpose of bringing a malpractice suit against a tribal witch doctor whom he considered to be a quack. After getting the broken stock mended, Seattle used the musket to send the witch doctor to the happy hunting ground.

Tolmie looked upon this as murder, threatening to hang Seattle from the highest tree at Fort Nisqually, but that was only one side of the story. By this time Seattle was Chief of the Suquamish and it was the chief's duty to eliminate medical men who were hiding too many of their mistakes in the *memaloose illahee*—the cemetery. He had gone to a lot of trouble and expense to perform his duty and he couldn't understand why Doctor Tolmie made such a fuss about it.

Violence brought Seattle considerable trouble in his personal life, but it was the basis of his success as a chief. Normally not very warlike, the Suquamish had always been pushovers for the Haidas on their summer raids and were even bullied by other Puget Sound tribes until Seattle taught them a thing or two.

When Suquamish spies brought word that River Indians —Muckleshoots—were planning a dawn foray down the Duwamish to attack his camp on Elliott Bay, Seattle decided to abandon the popular defense of running for the woods. Instead he loaded his toughest warriors into canoes and paddled upstream to where the overflow from Lake Washington joined the White River to form the Duwamish. The river was narrow there and the current swift. Seattle had his braves hack down a tall fir tree so that it spanned the stream a few feet above the water. Then they melted into the underbrush to polish up their war clubs.

Twenty canoe loads of hostiles came racing down the river that very night, so filled with happy anticipation of the coming slaughter that they failed to notice the missing fir tree. It was supposed to mark the edge of Seattle's private domain. The canoes were moving fast when they hit that fir tree and upriver braves were mowed down before they knew what had hit them. While they floundered about in the water, Seattle and his boys waded out with their clubs and proceeded to beat their brains out in the first game of water polo played in these parts.

After this Seattle capitalized on his reputation as an athlete and a military man to build himself a career in politics. His campaign resulted in a confederation of all the six quarrelling tribes around Elliott Bay with himself as leader.

Instead of fighting among themselves, the sub-chiefs moved into apartments at Seattle's headquarters, the Old Man House on Bainbridge Island, carving their family totems on their doorways and cooperating on a big thunderbird to go over the front door. They also cooperated in ganging up on their northern neighbors when they came down for their once profitable summer visits.

The Haidas were surprised and pained to discover that the traditional sitting ducks of Puget Sound had become thunderbirds with sharp claws. They were completely flabbergasted when Seattle led a flotilla of his allied tribes up north to clean out several of their villages and reverse the age-old grabbing process.

Violence having served its purpose, Seattle settled down to a life of respectability. It was the old patriarch who had long ago slugged his way to success whom the early white men knew. Maybe if they had known him as old Dr. Tolmie did—as the hell raisingest Indian in the Puget Sound country—they would have left his name alone and let him rest quietly in his Christian grave at Suquamish after he died in 1866.

But, on the other hand, there was a bit of wide open gambling and carousing as well as a fair amount of violence and sudden death in the youthful background of the highly respectable city that stole Old Man Seattle's name. Maybe that's why the Old Man's name seems to fit the town so well.

The Daily Times

DAILY SOCIETY
NEWS

In the Daily
Women's Department
See Page 10

N. WEDNESDAY EVENING, NOV. 25, 1903.　　　FIVE CENTS EVERYWHERE

PORTED SUNK IN COLLISION

ST B. F. DAY IS DISMISSED

AMITER BOUND FOR SEATTLE

DEAD AFTER LONG ILLNESS

OF SEATTLE START REVOLT

CHICAGO STRIKERS RETURN TO WORK

Employes Agree to Submit the Question of Wages to Arbitration.

Terms of Peace Do Not Require the Company to Recognize the Union.

Last of Seattle's Early Settlers Passes Away

DAVID THOMAS DENNY.

DAVID T. DENNY IS DEAD

Seattle's Oldest Pioneer Passes Away at Licton Park.

Sketch of the Life of a Very Remarkable Man.

DAVID THOMAS DENNY, one of the founders of Seattle, died at 2.30 o'clock this morning at the residence at Licton Park, near Green Lake. His wife and all of his children, one excepting and several of his grand-children, were at the bedside at the end, as was the Rev. E. Benjamin, pastor of the Green Lake M. E. Church.

ALKI MEANS BY-AND-BY

AFTER A WHILE that cabin out on the edge of the sea and the forest got a roof. The women had long ago stopped weeping; they were far too busy to weep. Even little Rolland Denny made out well enough. His mother was still too sick to nurse him and there wasn't a milk cow within sixty miles, but a friendly squaw had fed him a cupful of warm clam juice that first damp night in the roofless cabin and he had cried for more. It seemed to do him no harm and he became the first white child in history to be raised on clam juice.[1]

The Terry brothers were from New York and they were optimists. They saw a roof over their city and new cabins joining the first lonely one. After a while even the rain stopped and the mountains came out to shine above the blue waters of the bay. The Terry brothers decided that they had come to the right place after all, and that New York was a properly imposing name for it. Some day, surely, it would be the New York of the Far West.

Other settlers along the sound had the same idea about

---

[1] At any rate, Rolland Denny survived a trying babyhood on his clam juice diet and lived to fly in an airplane above the skyscrapers of the mighty city that had gone through its small beginnings wih him in a roofless cabin on a rainy beach.

16

their towns and they didn't take kindly to the Terrys' grandiose choice of a name. They showed their contempt by tacking a Chinook word onto it . . . *Alki,* which means by-and-by. The slower you drawl the word the further away that by-and-by becomes. The settlers from other towns *really* drawled it out, a procedure which annoyed the Terrys exceedingly.[2]

The pilgrims at New York Alki learned the Chinook jargon in self defense. The Indians were fascinated by the newcomers. They brought in portable houses to be set up on whatever ground was cleared by the settlers. They had never heard of the custom of knocking on doors. They just walked in complete with dogfish oil and dirt, and felt of everything that interested them. This included almost everything from babies to bread dough and one of the first Chinook words those early Seattle homemakers learned was *Klatawha!* That meant "Get the hell out of here".

One particularly fragrant Duwamish brave tried Mrs. Low's patience too far. Just when her bread was raising nicely on the hearth he stalked in silently and poked his dirty finger into the plumpest loaf. Mrs. Low grasped her wooden ladle, thrust it into a pot of boiling mush, and then whacked the savage violently across his bare behind. He departed with barbaric screeches and astounding rapidity, according to Mrs. Low's later accounts. She fully expected him to return with a scalping knife, but he never did. Instead she frequently saw him pointing her out to other In-

---

[2] The New York has long been forgotten, but the old contemptuous *Alki* has remained to designate one of the most beautiful districts of an unusually beautiful city. It was also adopted as the motto of Washington Territory, and a fitting motto it was for a commonwealth that was still growing up. Today few Seattleites are aware that the word has any particular meaning and practically none of them even pronounce it correctly. It's Al-key, but everyone in Seattle calls it Al-kie. A couple of generations ago almost everyone in town spoke a bit of Chinook jargon, but today the language is as dead as Sanskrit. *Kalakala* is a ferry boat and *Potlatch* is a community festival that was discontinued because it lost money and *Alki,* if properly pronounced, is something you used to get from your bootlegger during prohibition days.

dians, but always at a respectful distance, and apparently explaining to them that she was a dangerous woman and to be avoided at all cost. At any rate he never came back.

In the meantime, New York Alki had an industry as well as a roof and an imposing name. Less than a month after the landing from the *Exact* the brig *Leonesa* put into the bay. The brig's skipper was looking for a cargo of timber to take to California and the founding fathers were willing to accommodate him. The timber was right at tidewater. All they had to do was chop it down, lop off the branches and float it out to the ship.

That gave them the one thing they needed; a means of bringing a bit of cash money into town. It was a great thing for a city that was to be called Seattle, but it just about finished off New York Alki.

William Bell, the thoughtful old-timer of the party summed it up: " 'Pears t'me we've settled the wrong spot, boys", he announced soberly as the booted, flannel-shirted logging crew slogged through the dripping forest toward the little cluster of cabins. It was a raw day in early February and the noon rest—hot food and an open fire—would be a welcome relief from back-breaking labor.

Charley Terry, leading the party with his long-legged stride, whirled quickly, his dark eyes flashing. "What the hell do you mean, Bill? We all agreed on this spot and we've done right well so far—"

Bell swung his heavy ax from his shoulder to the ground and rubbed the small of his back, his easy grin flashing under his long, already graying beard. "Now don't rile all up, Charley", he rumbled soothingly. "We know you and Lee'r mighty attached t'New York, but facts are facts and we might's well face 'em like grown men".

The rest of the settlers had stopped too, and the male population of the new city formed a tight circle under the dripping trees. Bell raised his voice a little, talking to all of them. "We've found it's the harbor that's the means of providin' a living for us, hmm?"

The bearded men around him nodded slowly. The Terry boys were willing to agree to *that* much.

Bell's big calloused hand swept north and east in a wide gesture, taking in the great bay and the steep, wooded shores inland. "Take a look", he said soberly. "We need the harbor t'build a city, but we aint rightly *on* the harbor. We're way out on the tip of one of its breakwaters!"

Terry spat contemptuously and accurately at a fat black ant crawling on a shiny salal leaf, but Arthur Denny moved slowly up beside William Bell. "I think Bill's right", he said, his firm young face determined. "If the water's deep enough for sea goin' ships all the way in, the town should be *there* by rights." His lean finger jabbed toward the timbered heights to the east.

"How you figure on measurin' the water?" Terry asked contemptuously, "use young Dave here for a soundin' pole?"

David Denny flushed hotly. He was in love with Louisa Boren and hadn't had time to do anything about it yet, which made him irritable; furthermore, he was sensitive about his gangling youthfulness. "I know how we can measure it", he said quickly, "and I think Mr. Bell's right". With a quick twist of his arm he sent his glittering ax deep into a fallen log beside the trail. "I'll see you all right after lunch and I'll have the stuff to do the measurin' with", he promised. Then he turned and loped toward the glint of raw logs in the clearing ahead.

Mary Denny was dejectedly hanging clothes on the line outside the cabin and she shrieked when young Dave came hurtling through the wet brush behind her. "Lordy, Dave", she gasped when she saw who it was, "you nearly frightened me into a fit. It's bad enough trying to dry the wash for three children in this liquid sunshine without being scared to death by a young savage". Her pale face was warmed by a smile that belied her scolding, though, for Mary Denny was very fond of her young brother-in-law.

"I've got to have your clothesline, Mary", David panted.

Mary Denny's blue eyes twinkled. "If you're going to hang one of those pesky Indians I wish you'd wait till I get my cloak and bonnet".

"We've got no time for hangin' anybody", David panted.

"We're buildin' a new town". Mary Denny had been through a lot and, in her own way, she was a philosopher. She was already unpinning baby clothes from the hundred-foot length of cord.

She was still smiling faintly as David, the line coiled loosely over one arm, went sprinting back toward the beach. "Promise to bring it back!" she shouted after him. "It's the only clothesline in the whole town!"

David paused briefly at the forest's edge. "I know it, Mary. That's why I have to have it. I can't get the horseshoes from Charley Terry if he's got over his mad".

With this enlightening explanation he turned and was gone. Mary sighed and turned toward the cabin. Little Rolland was whimpering inside and she'd have to warm some clam nectar.

The Denny brothers, Boren and Bell paddled out in an Indian canoe that afternoon to take soundings of the harbor. The horseshoes at the end of Mrs. Denny's hundred feet of clothesline just didn't touch bottom any place they tried until the canoe was almost under the branches of the big trees on the eastern shore. If their clothesline had been twice as long it couldn't have reached bottom in most of the bay, but it was long enough to tell them that they had the makings of a seaport.

On February 15, 1852, the town moved to the eastern shore of Elliott Bay. It was a sad day for the Lows and the stubborn Terry boys, who were left alone with the thousand or so Indians who had moved in to enjoy the excitement and bustle at New York Alki. Those Indians probably had a lot to do with the willingness of the women to pull up stakes and start all over again.

The new town, which didn't rightly have a name yet (the Indians called the place "Skwudux", which would never do for a great city), got its first new settler when it was less than a month old. He was a dapper, jolly, handsome man in his early thirties and he came down from the south in a big canoe with Chief Seattle sitting beside him.

He was the best dressed man, and the happiest, that any of the settlers had seen since they left Portland and they drifted down from their cabin-building to watch him in a fascinated sort of way.

When he stood up in the canoe they could see that he was a well-built man, too, but he seemed to be swaying even more than the slim canoe. He pushed a tall beaver hat to the back of his head, revealing a high forehead and wavy brown hair. Then he pushed a pair of octagonal spectacles up on his forehead and surveyed the settlement and its gaping population. Seeming to like what he saw, he reached into the canoe, brought up a battered medical bag, opened it and extracted a green, square-faced whisky bottle with which he first solemnly saluted the shore, then raised to his smooth-shaven lips. On the stern seat beside him Old Seattle looked disapproving but resigned, like a loving father watching a favorite son making a fool of himself.

The newcomer surprised everyone, himself too, apparently, by clambering ashore without falling into the bay. He introduced himself as Doctor Maynard, Physician and Surgeon. He and Seattle were old friends and, more important at the moment, business partners, he explained. The chief's people were going to catch salmon for him and he was going to salt them down in barrels for shipment to San Francisco. Surely it would become a great industry. The founding fathers welcomed him.

The welcome must have warmed the heart of Dr. Maynard, for he had just been run out of the larger village of Olympia. Maynard was a physician, but having found the pioneers to be distressingly healthy, he had opened a store in Olympia. Now Doc Maynard was a handsome man and a well educated one, but he liked his nip of something to ward off the chill in winter and the heat in summer. It was only sociable to invite the customers of his store to share the nips with him. He had lots of customers, a fact which may be partly accounted for by his pleasant personality and partly by the fact that he was in the habit of lowering his prices with each drink. If there were enough customers and enough drinks he frequently ended up by giving his goods away.

Olympia, even in those days, had a somewhat smug and

stuffy character. Dr. Maynard's competitors, who stayed fairly sober most of the time, felt that his methods were unbusinesslike and unethical. In short, he was hurting their trade. They asked him if he would prefer to *Klatawha* out of town under his own power or astride a rail. He chose to go his own way in the canoe of his good friend, Chief Seattle.

Doc Maynard's salmon packing venture wasn't a success. His training had fitted him to cure people, perhaps, but not fish. After he had packed a thousand barrels the summer sun came out and the salt brine was too weak. The whole town smelled awful. Even the Indians noticed it. The whole season's pack had to be dumped in the bay and Doc Maynard went back to doctoring and storekeeping. His grand schemes for bringing a new industry to town didn't come to much, but at least one of his ideas caught on. It was Doc Maynard that thought of a proper name for the town.

Somebody had marked the name Duwamps on the map to designate the new settlement on Elliott Bay. Mail came addressed to Duwamps, Thurston County, Oregon Territory. Doc Maynard thought it was an awful name; reminded him of someone being sick to their stomach, he said. The founding fathers agreed with him, but it looked as if Duwamps it would be unless they took quick action. Maynard suggested the name of his friend and erstwhile business partner, Seattle.

The others weren't difficult to convince. Anything, they felt, was better than Duwamps!

So the town became Seattle and an old Indian of the same name went paddling sadly down the sound to the Custom House looking for a white *tyee* with authority to have it changed back to Duwamps or anything else in the world except Seattle. No one understood him. He was too proud to ever learn the bastard Chinook trade jargon and no one at the Custom House knew what he was talking about. Old Man Seattle forgave his white friend Maynard. His last request was that the Doctor come to his funeral and clasp his dead hand before he was buried, but he felt that a terrible injustice had been done him. He had been looking forward to peace and quiet in the Happy Hunting

Ground, but everyone knew that a dead man whose name was mentioned by the living was awakened by the sound. Peace and quiet indeed!

He would never have it now.

Quiet was a thing of the past for the town of Seattle too. It ended when a big, craggy man named Henry Yesler landed from another Indian canoe on the shore of Elliott Bay and walked up the beach to where the male population of Seattle was busy cutting timber. It was a place that, fittingly enough, is called Pioneer Place nowadays.

Henry Yesler didn't make a dramatic entrance as Doc Maynard had. Yesler was 45, which was an advanced age for a citizen of pioneer Seattle, and he was a man of substance as well as stature. He came of thrifty German stock and, as a skilled millwright, he had accumulated the wherewithal to build a steam sawmill. There wasn't a steam sawmill in all the Puget Sound country. It would be the makings of a real city. The founding fathers conferred together, leaning on their axes in the gently falling rain. Then they invited Yesler to build his mill anywhere he wanted to. They'd move over to make room for him.

Henry Yesler wasn't a man to be rushed. He'd sleep on it, if the town could provide a place for him to throw his blankets. The town could and did. Yesler spent the night at Arthur Denny's cabin and Mary cooked an extra good breakfast for him in the morning. After breakfast Yesler whittled a while on a piece of kindling wood, then said "Yah", he'd build his steam sawmill right about where he'd landed.[3]

The sawmill was built on the waterfront and the timber was skidded down a long panhandle of land from the wooded hills behind the town. The old skid road is Yesler Way on the city maps now, but the term *skid road* has stuck and spread to almost every big city in the United States, although in the East and in California it's been cor-

---

[3] The new town name appeared in print for the first time in October, 1852—in the Olympia *Columbian*. "Huzza for Seattle!" was the exuberant headline which announced the location of Mr. Yesler's new sawmill there.

rupted to Skid Row, a meaningless term the origins of which are lost in the mists of time and the steamy breath of Henry Yesler's sawmill.

The mill ran day and night, bringing ships to the bay and regulating the town's life by the shrill blast of its whistle. It gave employment to most of the male citizens and the more industrious of Old Man Seattle's tribesmen. The mill cookhouse, the last of the town's log buildings, was the social center of the region, and men who later owned banks and steamship lines and built skyscrapers on the hills were glad to roll out of their cabins in the pre-dawn darkness to answer the whistle blast and earn an honest dollar at Yesler's Mill.

The mill produced sawdust as well as lumber and even that wasn't wasted. Yesler hired a Dutchman named "Sawdust Ned" and set him to work with a big red wheelbarrow dumping sawdust to fill in the shoreline in front of Pioneer Place so that as the city grew the sea retreated to make way for streets and docks. It was a trend that was to continue and grow until Seattle had more reclaimed land that any other western city. Much of the city's present business and industrial districts are the result of the filling and dredging that began with the sawdust pile of Yesler's Mill.

The mill wharf became the landing place of the early Puget Sound steamboats, too, a fact which brought its share of confusion as well as prosperity. History records that a group of legislators, bound for Olympia on the *Eliza Anderson* were aroused one chill winter morning by what they thought was their steamer's whistle. Stumbling down the wharf in the rain and darkness, they were comforted by the sight of the open boiler room door with its promise of warmth and light.

Huddled around the boiler, they watched the fireman throwing slab wood into the firebox for some time. Finally one of them looked at his watch. It was past sailing time and he was sure they were still fast to the dock. He tapped the busy fireman on the shoulder. "May I ask when we are going to pull out for Olympia?" he inquired.

The fireman clanged shut the firebox door. "This sawmill don't run to Olympia, Mister", he observed calmly.

It was, they discovered too late, the wrong boiler room. The *Eliza Anderson* was gone and they had to make the voyage to the territorial capitol by Indian canoe.

Progress had come to Seattle and progress is always a confusing thing.

A BEAUTIFUL VISION FROM THE ASHES

RETROSPECT ON THE PAST AND PRESENT.

The Third Anniversary of Seattle's Great Fire.

June 6, 1889, is a date that will ever convey new that on that day a young city bright in ... sacrificed to glowing embers that fiercely the charred wreck of home and fortune, Seattle Phœnix of a new life. As from the ruins of ... from the entity, to the ... there arose a new the Pacific Northwest.

the sorrowful thought to the residents on Puget premises and strong in architectural ... raped to die in smouldering ruins. But even in proudly lifted her head and was infused with the Chicago there sprang a new and mightier Chicago, Queen City that today is the honor and glory of

The beginning of the fire is correctly depicted in the accompanying picture. The fire had its origin in a paint shop at the corner of Front and Madison streets. It traveled southward to the water front in a column where left swept along Second and Third streets, and where right licked up the docks, wharves and warehouses on the water front. The owls of the Occidental hotel block and Frye opera-house block, ... no idea as to how the city's commercial center disappeared as completely as though swept by a cyclone.

The "Old Sacramento," the first fire engine on the Coast, and which continues as an honored member of our efficient department, rendered valuable services. From 1876 until 1879 it was the only protection from fire they deemed that the day demanded.

THE BATTLE OF SEATTLE

THE YEAR 1853 brought important changes to Seattle. A year before the place had been Duwamps in Thurston County and its mail had been delivered to "Olympia, Oregon". It cost an extra twenty-five cents to have a letter brought down by the weekly canoe express. By the end of the year the address had become Seattle, King County, Washington.

The country north of the Columbia River had become a separate territory and there was word that a territorial governor was on his way out from the East, surveying the route of a transcontinental railway as he came.

In January David Denny and Louisa Boren were married in the evergreen-decked cabin which the bridegroom had built with his own hands on his claim out north of town. Radiant and lovely, as befitted Seattle's first bride, Louisa planted sweetbriar seeds, brought across the plains from home, around the cabin door and so Seattle got it's first flower garden, too.

The new territory boomed and Seattle boomed right along with it. Town lots studded with huge stumps and bordered by muddy trails began to sell for as much as two hundred dollars in hard money. Arthur Denny and Carsen Boren filed the first official plat of the city of Seattle on May 23, 1853. Doc Maynard had a plat of his own, but he staged a memorable drunk to celebrate the birth of the new territory and didn't get around to filing his plat until the next day.

Denny and Boren had laid out their streets parallel with the shoreline, but Doc Maynard was still the rugged individualist. *He* laid out his streets to conform with the points of the compass. The two plats met at Henry Yesler's skid road, but there was no meeting of minds between the platters. Doc was sobering up by easy stages and, as Denny asserted later, he was still carrying a sufficient head of steam to be convinced that he was not only master of all he surveyed, but of all Denny and Boren had surveyed as well.

That argument hasn't been settled to this day. The jog is still there where those two plats came together. North of Yesler Way the streets follow the original Elliott Bay beach; south of the old skid road they followed a compass course. And the original argument has been immortalized in the ever increasing snarl of traffic where all those mixed-up streets run into Yesler Way.

Traffic was no problem in 1853, however. Transportation was by what the pioneers called "Shank's Mare and Siwash Buggy", although that year of progress did bring the city its first wheeled transportation and its first steamboat. Tom Mercer brought his four motherless little girls to Seattle along with a wagon, a team of horses and a friend named Dexter Horton. The whole town turned out to hack a wagon road through the woods to the claim Mercer staked out on the lake called *Tenas Chuck* by the Indians —Lake Union in later years. It was Seattle's first road, built to accommodate the first wagon, so it was built narrow, but the settlers figured it was a step in the right direction.

Dexter Horton got a job at the new sawmill that was being built across the bay at Port Gamble. His wife joined him there to cook for the workmen, and when they made their stake they came back to Seattle to open a general store with the town's first bank as a sideline. Dexter Horton had an imposing iron safe, the only one in town, so everyone banked with him and sighed with relief when they saw their slim sacks of money stowed safely inside the iron monster. Banker Horton never worried about forgetting the combination to the town vault. If he did he would only have to go around behind. He had picked the safe up cheap because it didn't have any back. But a good front is the important thing in financial matters and the safe had that. Dexter Horton prospered and became one of the West's most famous bankers. The backless safe was the beginning of the Seattle First National Bank, the largest in the Northwest.

In addition to all the other gifts, the year 1853 brought a governor to newly formed Washington Territory. Major Isaac I. Stevens was a New Englander, small and peppery and full of very big ideas. He was making plans for a transcontinental railroad to connect his new territory with the rest of the United States and he was making plans to extinguish the Indians' claims to all the land in Washington Territory except such reservations as might be alloted to them. His railroad plans were badly tangled in governmental red tape, but he had full authority to act as Indian agent for a quick deal with the original owners of the Northwest country.

Stevens didn't believe in wasting time. He gave himself a month to cover the vast region west of the Cascades and north of the Columbia. He figured it would take the full four weeks to visit the thirty-odd Indian tribes, and a few minutes to "learn their needs" and place a valuation on their lands.

In the course of this whirlwind tour of the frontier the little governor stopped off at the village of Seattle to address the Indian population from the front door of Doc Maynard's log cabin drug store. He told them how much he loved Indians and how much the Great White Father at Washington loved Indians . . . so much that they were going to buy the Indians' land and move them to nice comfortable reservations where they would enjoy all the blessings of civilization including free vegetable seeds from the Department of Agriculture.

During the meeting the Indians swigged contentedly from jugs of blackstrap molasses provided by the government while the governor and his party nipped with equal enthusiasm from jugs which probably did not contain molasses.

The governor's love for Indians wore a little thin toward the close of the meeting when Chief Seattle took over the show. The chief executive was sensitive about his lack of height. Old Seattle towered a good foot above him and he didn't improve the governor's temper by putting the palm of his hand on the little man's head and keeping it there while he made a long and stirring oration. The governor is reported to have looked pained while this was going on . . . possibly because having Chief Seattle's hand on top of his head made him uncomfortable; possibly because Seattle made a better oration.

It ended up " . . . *At night when the streets of your cities and villages are silent and you think them deserted, they will throng with the hosts that once filled and still love this beautiful land. The White Man will never be alone. Let him be just and deal kindly with my people, for the dead are not powerless. Dead, did I say? There is no death, only a change of worlds"*.

That was in the early spring of 1854. Shortly thereafter little Mr. Stevens went hurtling back East to fight with Jefferson Davis over the route of his proposed transcontinental railway. For some reason Mr. Davis wanted it to run down south instead of over the northern route Stevens had picked out. Aware that he wasn't getting anywhere in that hassle, the governor was back again in November, all set to start moving Indians to reservations without any further delay.

He began turning out treaties the way they turn out mass produced automobiles in Detroit, but with one important difference. There's a lot of planning behind a Detroit production line. There wasn't enough planning behind Stevens' high-speed treaty making. Tribal chiefs were rushed through the ceremony of signing away their peoples' birthright and by the time the Indians began to realize what had happened to them the governor was miles away collecting other tribal signatures. And so the little governor scurried about happily, unaware that a storm of savage indignation was gathering in his wake.

The Indian War began east of the Cascade Mountains during the summer of 1855 while Governor Stevens was still busily making treaties. The Horse Indians began taking pot-shots at prospectors and one thing led to another. After a while the U. S. Cavalry was called out.

The summer passed quietly west of the mountains, but in September the Muckleshoot Tribe raided an isolated homestead in the White River Valley. The Muckleshoots had been thrown out of their traditional river homes and were to be moved into reservations with the salt water tribes. The Muckleshoots remembered the terrific beating Chief Seattle and his boys had given them when they came down the river in their war canoes and they had good reason to believe that the performance would be repeated if they were forced to move in with their traditional enemies.

The White River Valley settlers soon had enough of paint-smeared and war-whooping Muckleshoots. They abandoned their claims and fled to Seattle. Things were beginning to look serious. The citizens diverted a cargo of squared timbers for shipment to California and used it to build a blockhouse. While it was being built the town enjoyed its first visit from the United States Navy.

The sloop-of-war *Decatur* had come across from Honolulu under orders to "cruise the coast of Oregon and California for the protection of settlers". The skipper had fortunately allowed enough leeway in his orders to include Puget Sound in his cruise. The *Decatur* made her headquarters at Seattle. Stevens was in the Rocky Mountains by then, palavering with the Blackfeet while previous treaties were blowing sky-high behind him. Acting governor Mason kept urging the *Decatur's* skipper to go on about his business. He suspected that Seattle's founding fathers wanted the Navy in port for the purpose of providing trade for their stores rather than to defend them from Indians.

He couldn't convince the captain, but he did talk the White River settlers into returning to their claims. Arthur Denny tried to talk them out of it. He was getting private information from Chief Patkanim of the Snoqualmies, and what Patkanim said in effect was, "Stick close to the blockhouse, friend. All hell's going to bust loose before long".

The settlers went home at the urging of the acting governor. In October they were all killed—all but three children who were smuggled down the Duwamish River to Elliott Bay in the canoe of a friendly Indian. At Seattle the founding fathers formed a militia company and started for the White River Valley. The marauding Indians were gone, but they had left the mutilated bodies of the white settlers, all except those who had been cremated in their burning cabins. The volunteers buried the dead and returned to Seattle, more than a little thankful that they hadn't met up with the hostiles. Half the party's rifles were museum pieces that couldn't be fired and had been taken along only for appearance's sake. The blockhouse looked mighty good to them when they got back.

Seattle was attacked by the Indians on January 26, 1856, and the *Decatur,* which had been around all winter, almost failed to get into the show. While cruising off Bainbridge Island earlier in the month she had draped herself ungracefully across a then uncharted reef. On modern charts it's marked Decatur Reef in memory of that historic event.

The *Decatur* was somewhat rotten and decrepit at best and the stranding almost finished her off. She did, however, manage to wallow across the bay and beach herself on the mudflats by Yesler's wharf. The old girl had to be practically rebuilt from the waterline up. Her crew worked feverishly, day and night, while Indians gathered in the woods between Lake Washington and the town to whoop and screech and keep everyone awake nights. There were false alarms every night, some of them quite realistic.

On the night of January eighteenth the town was aroused by a woman's piercing scream and the loud report of a gun. Lieutenant Arthur Denny, in his nightshirt, led his volunteers to the blockhouse while the marines formed a line of skirmishers. After a while it was found that the Indians weren't involved. A sailor from the beached *Decatur* had tried to enter the bedroom of a village maiden by way of the window. The young lady had awakened and, with the piercing screech which had so alarmed her neighbors, slammed the sash down, pinning the unfortunate seaman half in and half out. Her 15-year-old brother had come running in response to her screams and proceeded to shoot the intruder through the head with a large charge of buckshot.

A few days later the comic opera aspects of the Battle of Seattle began working toward a climax. Into Elliott Bay steamed the survey ship *Active* with Governor Stevens aboard. He was back from the Blackfoot treaties and he still wasn't wasting any time. He came ashore and made a speech to the assembled citizens of Seattle. *"I say to you",* he concluded, *"that there are not fifty hostile Indians in this whole territory, and I believe that New York and San Francisco will as soon be attacked by the Indians as the town of Seattle".*

Then he scuttled off to the *Decatur* to try to talk the skipper into abandoning Seattle and going with him on a cruise to Bellingham Bay. Getting no response from either plea, he returned to the *Active* in a fine rage and departed without further delay. While the *Active* was still in sight in the bay, friendly Indians began coming into town looking for protection. They reported that large bands of hostiles had already crossed Lake Washington and were taking up positions for an attack on the town.

From here on it's not easy to pick truth from fiction. A cherished legend of Seattleites to this day has it that Princess Angeline, the daughter of Chief Seattle, crossed the bay in a dugout during a terrible storm to warn the city fathers of the impending attack. Another version has it that Doc Maynard's wife made the hazardous voyage disguised as a load of clams.

Lieutenant Phelps, the *Decatur*'s navigating officer, left the only written account of the proceedings, a highly imaginative document which critics have charged was written to divert attention from the navigation which resulted in his ship's stranding. It makes interesting reading even if it is fiction, but Seattle's pioneers didn't appreciate it. According to Phelps they were all cowardly yokels who were saved, in spite of themselves, by the U. S. Navy.

With all the warnings, real and imaginary, the citizens of the village were caught by surprise when the actual attack began. Most of them were eating breakfast in their cabins when the *Decatur's* howitzers began firing over their heads into the woods behind the town. The broadside was followed by much screeching from unseen Indians and the rattle of musketry. The population of Seattle abandoned breakfast and made a mass evacuation to the blockhouse. It was fast but orderly.

David Denny's pretty wife, Louisa, was alone in their cabin at the edge of town with her two-year-old baby. She had biscuits in the oven and when the firing began she scooped the hot biscuits into her apron with one hand, tucked the baby firmly under the other arm and was on her way to the blockhouse without a wasted second or a lost biscuit.

Mrs. Hanford had three small children to handle, but her mother, Mrs. Elizabeth Holgate had taught her that a pioneer lady must cope with emergencies in a dignified manner; furthermore, Mrs. Holgate had always set an example. Once when riding in a canoe which was swamped in a storm Mrs. Holgate had gained fame by remaining in it in an upright position with her bonnet firmly in place, apparently drifting ashore supported by nothing but water. On another occasion a large tree fell on her cabin, almost completely wrecking it. When horrified rescuers hacked their way in they found Mrs. Holgate calmly cooking dinner on the stove, which was practically the only thing in the cabin that had escaped destruction. Mrs. Hanford was a true daughter of Mrs. Holgate and she retired in good order with a small child under each arm. Her well trained son, Cornelius, who later became a noted judge, moved under his own power, but his training was almost too good. He returned to close the front door and was chased from the yard by a large Indian who rose suddenly from behind a log.

Out on the other side of town a Virginia gentleman with the romantic name of Hillory Butler was unable to find his pants. The way things sounded there was no time to look for them, so he made a dramatic entry at the blockhouse wearing his wife's red flannel petticoat. David Denny did only a little better. He snagged the seat of his homespun breeches as he tore through the brush and seemed more concerned with finding a secluded spot in which to repair the embarassing damage than in fighting Indians. Children dived in between the legs of marines and militiamen, frequently bringing them down with loud crashes. There were a few wild shots fired as a result, but no one was killed.

Fortunately the population was small and by the time the Indians had their muskets reloaded everyone was in the blockhouse or at least out of range and traveling too fast to hit.

Young Milton Holgate was in the blockhouse with the fowling piece that had protected his sister's honor a few nights before. He decided to try it out on an Indian. As he reached the doorway he received a bullet between the eyes. Later in the day a volunteer named Wilson made the same mistake with the same fatal result. Those were the only known casualties of the Battle of Seattle.

The *Decatur's* shells were disconcerting to the Indians. They had delayed action fuses which caused them to lie on the ground for a few seconds before exploding. The Indians said they *mox poohed*—fired twice—and they didn't like it. After a while they found that they had fired most of their own ammunition. They withdrew to have dinner and never really came back. The Battle of Seattle was over, but the citizens didn't know it for a day or two. Even then they kept expecting another attack, but it never came.

The legend makers took over as soon as the shooting stopped. Lieutenant Phelps reported that hundreds of Indians had come whooping across the sawdust pile at Yesler's mill to fire volleys at him and his men at a distance of *twenty feet*! Although their clothing was riddled with bullet holes none of them were scratched. He didn't say whether or not they suffered from powder burns.

Others solemnly asserted that they had seen Chief Seattle at the height of the battle performing a war dance on a sandspit in the bay.

The last shot of the Battle of Seattle was fired many years later. Gardner Kellogg, pioneer Seattle fire chief, had saved one of the *Decatur's* cannon balls as a souvenir. A quarter of a century or so later he was clearing stumps on his farm at the edge of town and decided to make use of the cannon ball. He rolled it into the fire which was burning under the largest of the stumps and went home for lunch. Dexter Horton, grown portly and prosperous as the town banker, then appeared on the scene. He was taking a noontime stroll and the fire looked good to him. He backed up to it and spread his coattails. The *Decatur's* shell warmed up at approximately the same time as the banker's backside. It *mox poohed* suddenly, blowing the stump in one direction and the banker in the other.

Banker Horton landed in a bramble patch with only his dignity seriously injured. Even the last shot of the Battle of Seattle was relatively harmless.

STEAMBOAT TOWN

DAVID DENNY had the right idea when he talked his sister-in-law out of her clothesline to use for sounding Elliott Bay. It was the harbor that gave Seattle its start toward becoming an important city. And it was the fleet of little Puget Sound steamboats that got people into the habit of traveling to Seattle to "do their trading".

Puget Sounders called it the "Mosquito Fleet", and it had its beginning in that highly progressive year of 1853. The Gove brothers had been running sailing ships in the California trade for some time. When they decided to branch out into the local steamship business they bought a tiny[1] sidewheel steamboat named the *Fairy* in San Francisco and shipped her north on their bark *Sarah Warren.* When the bark reached the sheltered waters of the sound the *Fairy* was lowered from the deck and filled with passengers for Olympia. She made it under her own power, although there were frequent stops along shore to pick up wood to feed her boiler fire.

The *Fairy* was greeted at Olympia by a cannon salute

---

[1] Mary Denny, taking her family to Olympia to visit husband Arthur, speaker of the Territorial Legislature, spread a feather bed on the *Fairy's* cabin floor to shelter the children. The feather bed filled the entire cabin.

and the loud cheers of the townspeople. November 12, 1853, the first Puget Sound steamboat schedule was printed. "The splendid steamer *Fairy*", it proclaimed, would make two trips a week between Olympia and Steilacoom and one trip a week between Olympia and Seattle. The fare was a modest five dollars for the 15-mile run between Olympia and Steilacoom and ten dollars for the 60 miles between Olympia and Seattle.

Seattle was proud to be a steamboat port, even though the fare was high, and everyone was sorry when the *Fairy* gave up the run after a few trips. She could make it from Yesler's wharf over to Charles Terry's dock at New York Alki in pretty good shape, but she just couldn't round Alki Point without scaring her passengers and crew half to death. Her owners decided to restrict her cranky movements to the sheltered waterway between Olympia and Steilacoom, a route which she continued to serve in a somewhat erratic fashion until October 22, 1857. On that fatal day she was pulling away from her Steilacoom dock in her usual uninspiring manner when her boiler went skyward in a spectacular explosion. No one was killed, but everyone aboard was more or less bruised and scalded except—of all people—the engineer. He escaped unscratched, but he was out of a job. The *Fairy* was seen no more and Puget Sound was all out of steamboats again.

That condition didn't last long, however. Steamboat owners were bound to respect people who were willing to pay ten dollars to ride 60 miles in a craft as slow, small and cranky as the *Fairy*. Soon steamboats were fairly flocking north from Portland and San Francisco. Some, like the *Fairy,* blew themselves up after short careers. Others sank, ran ashore in the fog or burned up. Others had long, profitable careers and became famous, like the *Eliza Anderson.*

The *Eliza Anderson* arrived in 1859 to run between Olympia and Victoria, B. C., by way of Seattle and intermediate points. Since her fares were almost as high as the *Fairy's* and she had the added advantage of a $36,000 a year mail contract she made a lot of money for her owners. People who knew her personally claim she moved slower and made money faster than any other boat in Puget Sound history.

Her progress was slowed down still more by the fact that her master, Captain Finch, ran a banking business on the side. Hard money was scarce in those days and Captain Finch made a good thing out of cashing drafts and the scrip issued by mills to their workers. By discounting such paper at a highly usurious rate the honest mariner established the foundation of a comfortable fortune. As long as there was a customer waiting the *Anderson* stayed tied to the dock.

The enterprising Finch had a steam calliope installed on the old sidewheeler's texas deck so people could hear her coming an hour or so before she got there. This attracted fleets of Indian canoes for the free concerts and warned prospective passengers and bank customers that it was time to be stirring.[2]

That calliope almost got the *Anderson* run out of Victoria, though. The ship's musician celebrated one Fourth of July in a number of Canadian bars and returned to the *Anderson* almost overflowing with patriotism at three o'clock in the morning. He fired up the calliope and proceeded to rend the pre-dawn air with a selection of American patriotic songs which brought hundreds of outraged Victorians bolt-upright in their beds. When the constabulary arrived at the dock the *Anderson* backed off into the harbor and lay there hooting "Yankee Doodle" at fifty pounds steam pressure to the square inch until the calliope player fell asleep on the keyboard and the concert ended in an ear-splitting wail from all the pipes at once.

It was an experience that Victoria was a long time forgetting.

In her old age the *Anderson* lost her lucrative mail run and was reduced to tramping around the Sound on lesser routes. One stormy night found the old sidewheeler making a desperate attempt to buck her way through Deception Pass. She was carrying a heavy load of freight and passen-

---

[2] The Old *Anderson's* famous calliope was later installed on another famous Seattle ship, the *Queen of the Pacific*.

gers. Included in the freight were seven pianos, eight head of cattle and a dozen barrels of whiskey.

Before long the old packet was getting water into her faster than the crew could pump it out. The skipper opened a pilot house window and roared, *"Overboard with the cattle!"* Into the water they went. Next came the order to dump the pianos. The whiskey and the passengers made it safely into Seattle. There the company agent visited the battered steamboat.

"Say, Cap", said he, addressing the *Anderson's* salty master, "don't you think you acted a little hasty in getting those pianos overboard and saving this whiskey?"

The skipper turned to him in utter scorn. *"Hell, man, you can't drink pianos!",* he roared.

The tough old *Anderson* lasted for nearly forty years and she was still raring to go in 1897. That was the year she joined the Alaska Gold Rush, trying to make it to Nome under her own steam. She made it as far as Dutch Harbor in the Aleutians, but there she ran out of coal and couldn't find any more. Her passengers and crew deserted her in the mad stampede to the Klondike and after a while she drifted ashore and broke up.[3]

By that time the Sound was filled with big and little steamboats, with most of them making Seattle their terminus. One of the most famous of them was the *Flyer,* a rakish single-stacker with a big triple-expansion engine and a slim knife-shaped hull. She was built at Portland in 1891, coming up to take over the Seattle-Tacoma passenger run shortly thereafter. She stayed on the run, off and on, until 1929 and literally millions of people followed the advice of her advertising slogan . . . *Fly on the Flyer.* By 1908 she had already made the equivalent of five trips to the moon or 51 voyages around the world, all on the 20-odd mile

---

[3] The old *Anderson* even had a part in keeping the territorial University of Washington solvent. In the 1860's University students were paid $1.50 a cord for cutting wood on the University campus. Captain Finch of the *Eliza Anderson* bought the wood for $2.50 a cord. This arrangement kept the old *Anderson* steaming and University students eating—and the profit was a mighty boon to the treasury of the struggling school.

course between Seattle and Tacoma. Before she was through she had rolled up more than two million miles.

Captain Everett B. Coffin was the *Flyer's* skipper during most of her career and he was a fitting master for a remarkable little ship. He was never known to turn down a race and even in her old age the *Flyer* was able to show a clean pair of heels to almost every boat on the Sound. Twenty years after her arrival in Elliott Bay she staged a spectacular race with the big steel packet *Indianapolis* between Tacoma and Seattle. It was on the last night run and the two steamers pulled out all the stops. With whistles blasting and bow waves like battleships they headed down Sound. They were carrying full passenger loads and every passenger was shrieking like a banshee.

It was a quieter world in those days and people could hear them coming for miles. The beach was lined with spectators all the way and half the town was down on the waterfront to see the racers in. Some say it ended in a dead heat. People who rode the *Indianapolis* say they won, but there are still people around town who rode the *Flyer* that night who will tell you the old champion was *never* beaten.

One thing is certain. Captain Coffin did his level best to inveigle Captain Penfield of the *Indianapolis* into another race, but the *Indian's* owners had issued strict orders; no more races with the *Flyer*.

The famous Sound speedster led a remarkably accident-free life, although she staged one disconcerting runaway early in her career. Captain Coffin was noted for his flying approaches to the dock, for he knew that he could bring her in at full speed and stop her almost in her own length when he rang for the engine to be reversed. It was old stuff to the *Flyer's* loyal passengers when she headed in like a hungry race horse at the end of her first afternoon trip from Tacoma on September 3, 1905.

At the last possible moment Captain Coffin gave the engineer a jingle for full speed astern. The engineer knew the skipper's habits and he responded without delay. He yanked the reverse lever hard over and walked over for a quick look out a side port. When he got there he was horrified to find that he was carrying the reverse lever with him.

A pin in the gearing had fallen out and the *Flyer* was still flying along at 18 miles an hour with an oyster company's dock coming up fast to meet her.

Captain Coffin had just time to stick his head out the pilot house window and shout a warning before his ship went through the dock. The dock warehouse went down for the count before the assault of the *Flyer.* Its floor opened up to dump several hundred dollars worth of unshelled oysters on top of the disturbed passengers. Several of them started to jump overboard, but were restrained in time. In spite of all the excitement no one was badly hurt.

Nobody was ever really hurt while travelling on the *Flyer,* although one tragic accident did befall a group of her prospective customers. A big crowd was waiting for her on a bright Sunday morning in May of 1912 when she arrived at Colman Dock. Hundreds were crowding around the gate when her gangplank was run out to meet the dock's loading slip and, as is usual in such cases, everyone tried to get on at once.

Just as the mass of humanity was packed heaviest on the gangway a cog broke in the mechanism holding up the moveable landing slip. The heavy plank structure fell from under the passengers' feet, one end dropping straight down to form a giant chute into the bay. At least sixty of the would-be voyagers skidded yelling down this slide, dropped through twenty feet of empty air and splashed into the scummy water below the dock. Those who hit the water last landed on the heads of those who went before them, and some survivors claimed that they went clear to the harbor bottom before they bounced back up.

Some of the *Flyer's* proverbial luck must have extended to her would-be passengers because only two persons were drowned in that churning maelstrom of struggling bodies.

Colman Dock was the hub of most of the Sound steamboat lines in those days, with scores of the little craft arriving and departing at all hours of the day and night for all the big and little harbors along Puget Sound's 2000 miles of shoreline. Practically everyone in town had occasion to pass through its big waiting room in pre-automobile days . . . particularly on Sundays after Seattle became moral and ordered the city's saloons closed on the Sabbath.

The steamboats' bars opened as soon as the dock was left astern, with the result that hundreds of thirsty Seattleites spent their Sundays shuttling back and forth between Colman Dock and Tacoma on the *Flyer* or *Indianapolis,* or Bremerton on the *H. B. Kennedy.* It was a custom that had its good points. The scenery was beautiful and most of the customers ended up seeing at least two of everything. Sometimes they fell overboard, or just stepped off the upper deck under the impression that they could fly like sea gulls, but little serious damage was done as long as the skipper stayed sober.

Such, it was charged, was not always the case aboard the big excursion steamer *Yosemite* which used to carry huge crowds from old Pier 6 at the foot of University Street. In 1908 she carried the whole student body of the University of Washington out to visit the fleet at anchor in Elliott Bay. The enrollment was smaller then than it is now, but it was still quite an accomplishment for one old side-wheeler.

The following year she was engaged in hauling excursionists to Bremerton for a look at the navy yard. On a July weekend evening in 1909 she was headed back for Seattle when, for some reason that has never been very adequately explained, she veered from her course and piled up on the rocks at the entrance to Port Orchard Bay. She was going full speed when she hit the beach and her big paddle wheels kept on turning helplessly long after she was impaled.

A rumor was wide spread that a blonde with a bottle in her hand had left the happy crowd of excursionists to tap invitingly on the pilot house window; that the *Yosemite's* skipper had forthwith left his ship to steer itself, but this interesting explanation of the *Yosemite's* sudden demise was never proven.

The passengers and crew of the *Yosemite* were all rescued by passing steamboats, after which the steward of the ill-fated craft (wrecked ships are *always* ill-fated) admitted to shoreside newspaper men that he had been the hero of the maritime drama. After the sickening crash (crashes at sea are *always* sickening) the steward stated modestly that he had sprung into action.

"This here pile-up panicked 'em, see", the steward explained modestly to the newshounds who had been sniffing all up and down the waterfront for a proper hero. (*All* shipwrecks must have a hero.) "So I calmly sits myself down at the piano in the grand salon and starts playin' soothin' music . . . Nearer My God To Thee, ragtime tunes . . . things like that there. Right away th' screechin' and hollerin' stops and everybody's saved".

The noble steward collected a large number of free drinks from the appreciative journalists and from other admirers along the waterfront on the strength of this story. His moment of glory ended, however, when the official inquiry into the wreck established the fact that he had sprung into action all right, but in an unheroic sort of way. The steward had been the third person to dive into a lifeboat and it was alleged that he missed first place only because he stopped briefly to kick an elderly lady who got in his way.

Boats still leave Colman Dock, but they're only ferry boats now—ungainly ghosts of the lusty little ships of the old Puget Sound Mosquito Fleet. They don't have bars, their skippers never challenge each other to impromptu Gold Cup Races and there isn't a steam calliope in the whole fleet.

It might be assumed that romance is dead on Puget Sound, but it isn't. All sorts of exciting things still happen, even on ferry boats. The young skipper of a famous streamlined night ferry which ran between Seattle and Victoria still wakes up screaming sometimes when he remembers one memorable voyage. Called below to quell what sounded like an incipient mutiny, he was confronted by a blonde beauty of abundant proportions whose only accessories, aside from those provided by a bountiful nature, were a choice Havana cigar and a high alcoholic content. Strolling the ship's corridors and puffing vast clouds of smoke from her cigar, this child of nature had created a remarkable uproar among her fellow passengers. There being no soothing piano available, the skipper was reduced to escorting the lady back to her stateroom and locking her in. The purser made heroic efforts to cover her with a draped blanket, but she haughtily shrugged it off, completing her pilgrimage as she had begun it . . . undraped.

The ferry boat is some 300 feet long, but the skipper said later that his nightmare journey down its corridors with the blonde seemed to cover many miles. Soon afterward he quit his job and took command of a freighter which carries no passengers at all.

Even more recently a lady school teacher, in some incomprehensible manner, was grasped and imprisoned by a popcorn vending machine on the steam ferry *San Mateo*. All efforts to free her were unavailing and it was necessary for the captain, chief engineer and crew to completely dismantle the machine before it could be made to disgorge the lady's hand and arm.

And even the prosaic motor ferries have enough of the old spirit left to scare hell out of their passengers by charging into Colman Dock at full speed occasionally.

When it happens the noise and confusion is just as satisfying as it ever was.

THE LEAN YEARS

THE BATTLE of Seattle had not produced many casualties as far as human lives went, but it was bad for the town and bad for most of the people who lived there. Town lots didn't sell for hard money any more, and timid souls who had expected Seattle to become a great city were shocked to find that it was, after all, just a frontier village that, but for the grace of God and the U.S. Marines, might well have been overrun by a mob of howling savages. They moved away. By 1860 there were only twenty families left in town.

Doc Maynard was among the hardest hit. He had always been a good friend to the Indians, a trait which had seemed amiable, but was now sinister. People who had once treated the bandy-legged Salish with reasonably good-natured contempt now hated all Indians and they hated "Indian-lovers" like Doc right along with them.

Doc was a Democrat, too, and the gathering clouds of civil war were bringing with them another term of contempt—*Copperhead*. Doc wouldn't compromise. He believed in state's rights and he made no bones about it even when he was sober, a condition which was becoming less and less frequent with him. All his old friends among the city fathers were Republicans. Doc Maynard, the most gregarious and open-hearted of men, felt himself rejected by

48

the town he loved. It was a situation that tended to sour Doc's usually jovial nature. On one occasion when he ambled over from his log cabin drug store to the new post office for his mail he found a group of settlers waiting outside the closed door. Doc, carrying a fine head of steam, plowed through them like a porpoise through a school of herring.

"No use hammerin' on the door, Doc", someone advised him. "Mr. Denny's a'sortin' th' mail. Won't let nobody in till he's got it ready".

"Well now by the rosy pink behind o' th' prophet", the enraged doctor bawled, "it appears to me that Art Denny's got powerful big fr' his britches since he got appointed post master!" With that irate pronouncement he kicked down the rough board door and walked over it a bit unsteadily to the pigeon-hole where his mail was kept.

Arthur Denny peered quietly at Doc from behind a fanned-out deck of letters and folded newspapers, but he said nothing as Maynard collected his copy of the Olympia *Pioneer and Democrat* and a scattering of bills and letters. Maynard moved toward the doorless opening of the post office in silent dignity, then thought better of it and turned to the quiet post master. "I don't suppose an important official of the Whig government like you'll take an outrage like this lying down. If you want t'make something of it the sheriff knows where t'find me".

Denny's slow smile answered the doctor's angry challenge. "I'd say you got your politics out of a bottle this mornin' Doc", he said pleasantly, "and that bein' the case, I'm prepared to take most anything from you except pills".

Doc snorted like an angry grampus, but Denny continued good naturedly, "There's a temperance lecture goin' on at Yesler's hall t'night. It might do you good".

"Temperance!" Doc roared. "That's the only thing I believe in taking in moderation. In fact I'm total abstainer". With that parting blast he strode majestically from the post office and through the crowd of gaping onlookers.

Twenty minutes later a carpenter, hired by Doc, appeared on the scene to replace the broken door, but Doc never apologized formally.

Doc Maynard further scandalized Seattle when it developed that he had two wives. He had left one in the East under the impression that she was to be summoned when her husband had established himself on the new frontier. But Doc fell in love on the Oregon Trail. The girl was Catherine Broshears, sister-in-law of Big Mike Simmons who had founded the city of Tumwater at the southern tip of Puget Sound. Big Mike didn't approve of the romance and Doc suspected that he had given undercover support to the movement which resulted in Doc's retreat to Elliott Bay in Chief Seattle's canoe.

Obstacles only got Doc's dander up and after fast-talking the Territorial Legislature into granting him a divorce from his first wife—an act of great convenience but doubtful legality—he proceeded to woo and wed the charming Widow Broshears.

It was fine when Doc brought Catherine to Seattle, but it was confusing when his first wife, tired of waiting, turned up there also. Uncle Dan Bagley, the Methodist minister, shook his shiny bald head and waggled his fine white chin whiskers sadly when he heard the news, but he liked Doc, just as everyone else did, and he tried to find excuses for him. "After all", he admitted, "I've searched the Bible and I can't find a single passage that actually forbids a man to have more than one wife".

But Doc exploded that one himself when it got to him. "How about the one that says 'No man can serve two masters'?" he asked ruefully.[1]

In the end Doc managed to settle his marital difficulties in his old amiable manner, the two ladies sharing the same house while things were worked out, but it all aided in his downfall. He had staked half his claim on Seattle in the name of his first wife. When it was decided that his second wife, Catherine, was his lawful spouse it meant that half his land was held illegally and it reverted to the government. Doc, a true one-man chamber of commerce, had already given much of his land away

---

[1] Mark Twain used this one in 1889, Milton Berle in 1952.

to help the city grow, so this newest calamity left him with only a fraction of the property that had been his and which today is worth something well over a hundred million dollars.

He traded what was left for Charles Terry's claim out at New York Alki. Terry thus salvaged some of the ground he had lost through misplaced loyalty to that original settlement, while Doc was probably no worse off than he would have been anyway. More and more he was viewing a topsy-turvy world through the distorted glass of a whiskey bottle.

The Terry place was comfortable enough—a big white clapboard house with many-paned windows of real glass and fireplaces built to take whole driftwood logs from the beach just beyond the front yard. But it was a farm house and Doc was no farmer.[2] Mud and manure weren't for him; besides, a man who's up most of the night working his way through a demijohn of blue ruin whiskey is seldom in shape to start milking cows and plowing ground at sunup. That was one of Doc's troubles.

Another was his childlike generosity, which didn't make any reservations. Anybody who showed up at Alki Point —A. W. O. L. sailor, itinerant actor, patent medicine quack or begging Siwash was a guest as far as Doc was concerned and a guest deserved the best there was in the house.

After a while it got so there wasn't much in the house for Doc or his guests either. Word got around across the bay that Catherine was digging clams on the beach three times a week, and in pioneer Seattle circles that meant just one thing . . . poverty.

Catherine remained staunchly loyal to her handsome,

---

[2] Some idea of Doc's farming ability can be gained from the contemporary account of an old gentleman named David Stanley. After looking over Doc's Alki property, old man Stanley announced that the experience had given him religion. "Nothing short of the ingenuity and power of the Almighty could have piled up as many logs and stumps to the acre as I found on your farm," he told Doc.

impractical husband.[3] So did his old fishing partner, Chief Seattle, who sometimes came across the bay on summer evenings, wrapped in his blanket toga, to palaver with his *tilikum,* the *Doctlin.* Some folks, newcomers mostly, viewed Old Man Seattle's visits with scorn. "Doc's got so low-down and no account he's taken to drinkin' with dirty old Injins", they sneered. But the old-timers knew better. Old Man Seattle had long ago renounced the ways of his wild youth and he would drink only well sweetened coffee. He didn't approve of Doc's heavy drinking, but disapproval didn't affect his loyalty. Being only a simple Indian he figured that friendship was something stronger than blue ruin whiskey.

Old Man Seattle's loyalty to Doc Maynard was as strong as ever, but the rest of his strength was gone. The chief who had formed a great Indian confederation was no longer a man of power. He was living out his days in the crumbling Old Man House, the totem-carved labyrinth that had once been the headquarters of his Indian nation. He was collecting the rewards of loyalty to the white men, which meant that he was slowly dying of hunger and neglect. His last oration was a plaintive echo of the vital, throbbing prose that had carried him to unheard-of leadership among the Indians of Puget Sound . . .

"I fear that we are forgotten—or that we are cheated of our lands. I have been very poor and hungry all winter, and I am very sick now. In a little while I will die. I should like to be paid for my land before I die . . ."

Seattle's wish was not granted, and when the Old Chief died, Doc Maynard went across the bay to Agate Pass. There, on the beach below the dark labyrinth of the Old Man House, he shook the dead hand that had been extended to him in friendship so long ago.

---

[3] She planted a herb garden in back of the house to grow the things Doc needed to brew his frontier remedies, even sewing a packet of dandelion seeds from the East in order to have the ingredients for dandelion tonic. There were no dandelions in the Puget Sound country until then, and all the ubiquitous yellow-crested weeds that plague the keepers of neat lawns to this very day are descendants of Doc Maynard's herb garden dandelions.

A quarter of a century later—in 1890—the respectable people who had known Old Man Seattle got around to paying their tribute to him. Henry Yesler and other city fathers bought a handsome monument to be erected over his grave at Suquamish. But if, as Seattle had feared, he was wakeful under the shaft of Italian marble, he probably wasn't much impressed by all the stir. He had never cared for the white men's *ictas,* so coveted by his lesser tribesmen. He had been impressed with the warm, human gifts of a drunken village doctor who died broke.

Seattle's daughter, Kick-is-om-lo, known by the white population as Princess Angeline, lived on in a junk-crammed shack on the town's waterfront between Pike and Pine. Uglier than sin and possessed of little of her father's dignity, Angeline became a town character, peddling clams and firewood and sometimes scrubbing floors for the more prosperous housewives. The boys of the town delighted in the perilous sport of taunting Angeline and then dodging, if they could, the rocks or hard-shelled clams which she flung like a big-league pitcher. But when Angeline died, just before the turn of the century, Seattle children bought the monument that marks her grave in Lake View Cemetery and came to strew flowers on it after the funeral.

As for Doc Maynard, he never quite lost his fighting spirit or his sense of humor. One day a very young and nervous couple landed from a canoe on his beach at Alki Point. Doc couldn't recognize them at that distance, but of course he bawled an invitation for them to come up to the house. There they informed him that they had come up from Olympia, stealthily and by night and for just one purpose. They wanted to get married . . . had run away from home, as a matter of fact. Doc knew the boy; they were kinfolk. He was young Christopher Columbus Simmons, son of Mike Simmons. Mike had been one of the first Americans to reach the Puget Sound country back in 1846. Young Chris had been born on the Columbia River during the course of that migration. Furthermore, Mike Simmons was one of the respectable businessmen who had helped run Doc out of the Upper Sound country. Still further, Mike Simmons was the brother-in-law of Doc's second wife and he had done everything he could to discourage Doc's courting.

Doc was torn between his natural sympathy for true love combined with his human desire to put one over on Big Mike Simmons, and his conviction that this girl looked extremely young. "How old is she, boy?", Maynard asked young Simmons confidentially. "Thirteen", the boy admitted, but they were sure they loved each other and they were going to get married one way or another.

Doc figured they might as well do it legally, all things considered, and after a drink or two to warm up his thinking processes, he came up with a brilliant scheme. He wrote the figure "18" on two pieces of paper and requested the bride to humor him by putting one in each shoe. Then he went with them to Seattle and the residence of the Reverend Daniel Bagley for the ceremony. Doc agreed with the minister that the girl looked a mite young, but declared that he was willing to swear, on the Bible if necessary, that she was as he put it, "Over eighteen".

The young couple were duly joined in matrimony before a posse of angry parents arrived on the scene. Mike Simmons was no more amused by Doc's simple stratagem than he had been when his sister-in-law's heart had been carried by storm, but there wasn't much he could do about it. The affair didn't enhance Doc's reputation for stability, but even after sixty years and more Chris Simmons remembered that day with gratitude. Along about 1920 he issued a sort of informal progress report: *"We have at present in our family sixty, including ourselves, children, grandchildren and great-grandchildren".*

Doc Maynard seldom made a mistake when it came to other folks' welfare. He seldom made anything but mistakes when it came to his own.

After a few years at Alki the Maynards' house burned down and Doc returned almost thankfully to the town he had always loved. He opened a hospital and drug store and he hung out his shingle as a lawyer. He kept drinking; folks said "Old Doc's a better doctor drunk than the rest of them cold sober", but they seldom thought to pay him for his services and Doc hated to send bills. One of the last things he did was to deed one of his few remaining tracts of land to the Masonic Lodge for a new cemetery.

He died a few months later, an event which prompted every soul in town to remember that they had loved Old Doc all the time, even when he was acting orneriest. The whole town came to Yesler's Hall at First and Cherry to say goodbye to Old Doc.

But, as always, Doc Maynard was ahead of his time. He was to be the first to be laid to rest in the new cemetery he had given to the town, but it wasn't dedicated yet. His body lay in the tool shed at the old cemetery—Denny Park now —until the plot at the new one was ready for him.

Mother Damnable was another pioneer who never quite got over the Battle of Seattle. Her real name was Mary Ann Conklin, but the town knew her by the title her tongue had earned for her. There were two hotels in Seattle in the 1850's, the two-story white clapboard Felker House, which was the primitive forerunner of the Rainier-Grand and the Olympic. Mother Damnable ran the other one.

No one was quite sure about her background, nor was anyone tempted to ask. Mother Damnable was large and grim of visage. She kept a pair of savage Indian dogs tethered in the back yard of her hotel and a big pile of stones in front. Those who aroused her wrath were likely to find themselves under simultaneous attack by dogs, stones and Mother Damnable's tongue. The dogs and stones were bad enough, but it was the lady's language that made her feared and respected. It was said that Mother Damnable's profanity was of a quality never heard before or since in the Northwest. It was an irresistible blast before which stolid Indians blushed a deeper red, paint peeled from buildings and the toughest frontiersmen quailed and fled.

When the *Decatur* came to protect Seattle from the Indians, Mother Damnable hung no welcome signs in the windows of her hotel. She let it be known in violent terms that she preferred painted savages to prowling sailors and she backed up her prejudice with aprons-full of rocks, unleashed dogs and veritable epics of profanity.

Her wrath reached a crescendo when shore parties from the *Decatur* began constructing a road across the front of her property. Her whole arsenal of weapons came into play with the result that the Navy retired in disorder. In vain did the imaginative Lieutenant Phelps try to explain that they were building the road to drag the ship's howitzers across town for the proper defense of Seattle and the protection of its female population from a fate worse than death at the hands of the redskins. Mother Damnable wasn't having any of that. She chased Lieutenant Phelps away too.

Other parties were sent to replace their fallen comrades, but none were able to stand before the onslaught of the determined lady. They tried wiles and strategy, but all to no avail. Days passed and no progress was made on the hotel sector of the howitzer road . . . until a hardbitten old petty officer from the *Decatur* came ashore and took a look at Mother Damnable as she passed him in full cry and rock-filled apron in pursuit of his comrades. He delved into his gaudy memories and came up with a recollection of Mother Damnable in other days—when both of them had been considerably younger and she had been a notable resident of one of the East Coast's better known districts of ill repute.

He planted himself in the unfinished roadway and met her upon her victorious return. Mother Damnable reached into her almost depleted apron for a rock. Then a look of dawning recognition crossed her craggy face.

The quartermaster saw his advantage and immediately took the offensive. "So this is where you ended up from screechin' hell and damnation around Fell's Point in Baltimore, you damned old harridan", he roared. "A fine sight for an honest sailorman *you* are, aint you?"

Mother Damnable knew that most of Seattle had been witnessing her forays from safe distances, but not far enough away to miss hearing the quarterdeck voice of her accuser. Her carefully guarded past was public property now. She let the rest of the rocks fall from her apron and used it to cover her head. She retreated to her hotel and the *Decatur's* men saw her no more. They finished their road in comparative peace and quiet with only the whooping of hostile Indians in the woods to distract them.

As for Mother Damnable, she did not long survive her

public defeat. She gave up the ghost quietly enough and was buried in the old Seattle Cemetery. After Doc Maynard gave the town its new burial ground the old one was abandoned. Then in 1884, its owner, David Denny, turned Seattle Cemetery over to the city to become its first public park. The bodies of the pioneers were to be removed.

All went well until the workmen uncovered the coffin of Mother Damnable. This one they couldn't lift at all. They called for reinforcements, as the Navy had once been forced to do, but still it couldn't be budged. Those who had known her wondered if perhaps she was still gathering rocks in her apron, but when they rigged a hoist and lifted the coffin out—it weighed nearly half a ton—they found that Mother Damnable had turned to rock entirely. The coffin contained a mighty image of petrified stone.

Old Seattle Cemetery became a park, as had been planned. In later years when the hill under it was washed into the tideflats in a great regrade operation the park was rebuilt on a lower level where it exists today as an oasis of green in the heart of an expanding city.

But the thing that impressed the pioneers most was not the park or even the fact that indestructible Mother Damnable had turned to stone. The thing that amazed them was this: when they opened her coffin Mother Damnable was smiling a pleasant and satisfied smile.

It was the first time anyone in Seattle had seen her looking happy.

PURE YOUNG LADIES, AND OTHERS

IN THE BEGINNING Seattle had been just a few scattered cabins in the forest, each family working its own claim with little time or energy for civic doings. Afterward the Indian War stopped all community progress for several years, but the 1860's ushered in a new period of development. The town had a newspaper, the *Argus,* which carried the advertising of such old stand-bys as D. Horton's Staple and Fancy Dry Goods Emporium, Charles Terry's Eureka Bakery and Yesler, Denny and Company's Lumber and Flour Mills. The youth of the town could drink sarsaparilla at Gardner Kellogg's Drug Store, and the aged were comforted by Kellogg's Golden Balm. If that sovereign remedy failed, Shorey's Undertaking Parlors were available.

University students, forbidden to attend "balls, saloons and theaters", could still have a fling at the frequent church socials or listen to the brass band in the summer time. And there was always the community Christmas celebration at Yesler's Hall, with stout old Henry Yesler himself as florid and beaming and hearty a Santa Claus as any child could ask for.

But there were a lot of things Seattle still needed in the 1860's; new settlers to replace those who had been scared away by the Indian War, industries to augment the old

59

steam sawmill down on the waterfront, and the railroad that Governor Stevens had promised back in 1853, but most of all Seattle needed women. There were ten men to every woman in the Puget Sound country. A girl who passed her sixteenth birthday without being married was considered an old maid.

Most of Seattle's male population was young, virile and lonesome. A few fortunate ones were able to coax an eligible white maiden to Uncle Dan Bagley's parsonage for a wedding ceremony, but the vast majority had only two alternatives. They could substitute vigorous wood-chopping and frequent cold plunges in Puget Sound for thoughts of the gentler sex, or they could take up with an Indian maiden.

This wasn't difficult, since sexual morality was not stressed in the Salish culture, but it had its drawbacks. Most of the Indian girls were distressing to look at, at least by white standards which did not set a premium on bow legs, flattened skulls and excess weight. Most of them did have luxuriant and glossy tresses, but since they achieved this result by frequent shampoos in urine followed by a fish oil rub, it failed to add much to their general desirability.

True, a few determined settlers took the time to thoroughly cleanse and renovate a squaw, but it was such a tedious process that most of those who accomplished the feat were reluctant to part with the purified damsel. A good many of these interracial alliances lasted a lifetime, some of them even developing into regular *Boston* style marriages, but still the basic problem remained. There just weren't enough women to go around.

Two young men took steps to remedy this aggravating situation, each in the manner which seemed most reasonable to him. The results were widely divergent, but both left permanent imprints on Seattle history. One was named John Pennell; the other was Asa Mercer.

Pennell answered Seattle's call from the Barbary Coast of San Francisco where he was operating an only moderately successful brothel. Competition was fierce in San Francisco, but a quick trip to Seattle on a lumber brig convinced him that there would be no competition at all there.

He would be in the enviable position of maintaining a monopoly in a town with lots of potential customers and a steady payroll.

Within a month of Pennell's arrival Seattle's uninspiring skyline had been augmented by a large rectangular building of rough lumber on the sawdust fill just south of Yesler's mill. It was the first structure of its type in this area . . . or in all the Puget Sound country for that matter . . . but it was far from the last, and it set a pattern for those that were to follow.

It had a board floor for dancing, a bar for drinking, and a number of small, cube-like rooms for privacy. It was staffed at first by well scrubbed and copiously perfumed Indian girls, but as it prospered Pennell imported a number of badly wilted blossoms who couldn't find employment for their talents in San Francisco.[1] Seattle had the only establishment in all of Washington Territory employing white women in the oldest profession. It also had a topic of debate among its leading citizens. It was a controversy that wasn't settled for sixty years or more and was destined to give Seattle city politics a schizophrenic tinge almost unparalleled among American cities.

One faction of the solid citizenry was all for running Pennell and his bevy of bedraggled beauties out of town and setting fire to his establishment, which was known familiarly as the Mad House. Others deplored the evils of the place, but pointed out that it *did* draw its clientele from all over the territory, it was putting Seattle on the map as nothing else ever had, and at least some of the dollars brought to town by Pennell's customers were finding their way into the tills of honest business men.

Some historians solemnly assert that John Pennell's Mad House on the sawdust pile was the factor that tipped the scales in favor of Seattle as the undisputed metropolis of the Northwest. Olympia was a larger city, but the stuffy

---

[1] An exception was Pennell's star attraction, a buxom lady called "Flying Cloud", who is said to have had an exact reproduction of the famous clipper ship of the same name tattooed on her stomach. *She* would have done well in any seaport.

character of the place which had repelled·Doc Maynard
had been enhanced by its selection as the territorial capitol.
When folks had money to spend . . . menfolk at any
rate . . . they headed for Seattle to spend it; a habit
which never changed with the years, even after the original
attraction had been long forgotten.

The Mad House begat its crop of legends, among them
tall tales of damsels who moved from its sordid rooms to
neat houses on the hill—and eventually to ornate Victorian
mansions as the city and the fortunes of their husbands
grew. If the legend is true, as it well may be, no leading Seattle families boast of their descent from the Pennell Girls.

A number of them are proud to claim great-grandmoth-
ers who were imported by Pennell's contemporary, Asa
Mercer.

Young Asa was the much younger brother of Tom Mercer, who had brought Seattle its first horse and wagon. His
parents had followed Tom across the prairies and the
mountains to the promised land and Asa was born on the
migration—in Illinois. Tom was 25 years old when his
brother Asa was born.

Asa's first recorded employment was in clearing brush to
help make the University of Washington Territory campus
and, later, as a carpenter during the construction of its first
building. Uncle Dan Bagley, the Methodist minister, had
conspired with Arthur Denny to get the University for Seattle. Its site was considered a political plum by the Territorial Legislature, which was in the habit of awarding it to
a new and hopeful settlement each session. When Seattle's
turn came it horrfied the lawmakers by actually building
the institution before the legislature could meet again and
award it to some other town.

Denny not only guided the move through the Legislature
—he was speaker of the house—but he arranged to have
Bagley appointed president of the University Commission,
and then gave ten acres of land for the campus. The legislature had appropriated two townships of land to finance
the University, having taken the precaution of setting the
sale price well above the market value. Bagley and Denny
could remember the days of barter when there wasn't any

hard money. They traded land for lumber at Yesler's mill. Workers were offered two acres of land for a day's work.

Even with that kind of arrangement, some cash was needed, however, and Bagley solved that problem, too. The politicians at Olympia figured it would be impossible to sell the two townships of University land when the price was higher than that of any other government land, but they had forgotten one thing. Those two townships could be selected from any unoccupied part of the public domain. Prospective buyers were offered their pick of the choicest land available, with the result that the University's promoters literally did a land office business.

Within nine months of the Legislature's gracious but meaningless gesture in giving Seattle an imaginary university it was there in solid reality, an imposing white-columned structure with a domed cupola, on the hill above the town. The scattered weekly newspapers of the territory carried notices that the Territorial University would open its doors on November 4th under the supervision of Rev. Daniel Bagley, President of the Board of Commissioners. The president of the institution—its entire teaching staff, as a matter of fact—was Asa Mercer.

The Legislature was properly outraged when its members learned of Seattle's enterprise. They felt that the building of the University was premature and that Seattle's behavior was downright grabby. It was a charge that less fortunate communities were to be making against Seattle for many years.

An investigating committee was sent up from Olympia. The members, met at the dock by the brass band and given Seattle's best V. I. P. treatment, inspected the neat white building on its well-cleared campus; then reported back to their colleagues that things seemed to have been taken out of their hands. Legend has it that it was this group of bemused lawmakers who wandered into the engine room of Henry Yesler's sawmill under the impression that they were boarding the *Eliza Anderson* for the return to Olympia. Thus they provided Seattle with a good laugh, but that was all. The Legislature refused for many years to appropriate any funds at all for the support of the University.

Seattle refused to admit that its University was premature, but even Bagley and Mercer had to concede that there were no high school graduates in the territory looking for a college education. The classes were limited to elementary and grammar grades and the first college class of one wasn't graduated for another fifteen years.[2]

Lack of funds kept the school term short, so President Mercer had plenty of time to look around and consider Seattle's other needs. He was aware of Mr. Pennell's Mad House on the beach south of the skid road. Nobody could ignore its presence on a Saturday night when the loggers and sailors were in town relaxing, but Mercer didn't think it was the proper solution to Seattle's most pressing problem. It occurred to him that with the male population of the East engaged in killing itself off on the battle fields of the Civil War there must be a surplus of pure young ladies of high intelligence and moral character in those parts. It seemed reasonable to him to import this surplus to a place where it would be appreciated; namely Seattle.

Territorial officials favored the plan. Many of them were lonesome bachelors themselves, but there just wasn't any money in the public treasury for such an enterprise. Mercer decided to put his campaign on a personal basis. He travelled about the area with a highly attractive sales pitch: "Let me have the price of a girl's passage out from the East," he suggested slyly, "and the chances are she'll be so grateful that she'll marry you in a hurry when she gets here . . . before the rest can start courting her".

The young men of Washington Territory were suspicious at first. This professor Mercer dressed like a dude and had such polished manners that he reminded them of a slick gambling man. He admitted that his proposition *was* a gamble, in a way, but the stakes were mighty attractive.

---

[2] The University of Washington was still pretty much of a shoestring operation in the 1890's. President Eliot of Harvard, meeting a University of Washington professor of that era inquired what chair he occupied. "I teach botany, physics, astronomy, psychology, zoology, anthropology—" the professor began. "My dear fellow," Eliot interrupted—"You don't occupy a chair; you occupy a settee!"

Mercer left for the East with a bulging wallet. Arriving in the New England states early in 1864, he was almost mobbed by pure young ladies who wanted to start a new life in the Great Northwest. Elated, he sent a dispatch to Seattle announcing that he would soon be on his way with at least fifty of the youngest and purest; that hundreds more were available next year.

Professor Mercer was a very young man, for all his luxuriant side whiskers and book learning. He failed to properly appreciate feminine nature. When sailing time came most of the girls announced that they simply didn't have a thing to wear or they just hadn't had time to pack. All but eleven dauntless maidens changed their minds at the last moment and decided to wait for the next boat.

The little party left New York in March of 1864, travelling by way of the Isthmus of Panama to San Francisco. There they boarded the bark *Torrent* which carried them to Port Gamble. From there the sloop *Kidder* took them across the Sound to Seattle, where they arrived near midnight of May 16th.

The hour was late, but news spread fast in pioneer Seattle and Yesler's wharf was jammed with hopeful males. There were a lot more than eleven cash contributors in the crowd, but instead of lynching Mercer they elected him to the Territorial Legislature in gratitude for the modest accomplishment he *had* made and in the hope that he would return for another shipment the following year.

As for the pioneer Mercer Girls, all were offered genteel employment, but few of them needed it. All but one were married or spoken for by the following spring. History records that only a Lizzie Ordway remained permanently a spinster.[3]

The war ended the following year, which gave Asa Mercer a really big idea. He was aware that every port on the eastern seaboard was jammed with government ships, their

---

[3] The most diligent research has failed to unearth a picture of this unique young lady, which is probably just as well, but it is known that she was Seattle's first public school teacher and a leader in the Woman Suffrage movement.

bunkers full of coal and their 'tween decks full of sailors who were eating their heads off at government expense and doing nothing. He recalled that, as a small boy in Illinois, he had sat upon the lap of Abraham Lincoln and listened to certain of the less pungent of his funny stories. He was sure that the President would be a sympathetic ally in his plans to borrow a government ship to transport respectable war orphans to a land where they were assured of good homes and almost overwhelming appreciation.

Mercer made a quick survey of the situation. His 1864 importation hadn't altered things any. It had been like trying to put out a forest fire with a sprinkling can. "There is not a single woman of marriageable age on Puget Sound or the inlets north of Olympia", he reported, "save two or three school marms who accompanied me from the East last year, and they are all preparing their wedding trousseau".

Mercer wasted no more time. He boarded a ship for New York, and he arrived there on April 14, 1865. It was early evening, but there was no train leaving for Washington until the next morning. He checked in at a New York hotel at about the time President Lincoln was leaving the White House for Ford's Theater where a mad actor named John Wilkes Booth was waiting.

The national capitol was draped with black crepe when Mercer arrived the following evening. It matched his mood perfectly. "I was at sea without a compass", he admitted afterward. But he kept going. The Governor of Massachusetts was sympathetic to his scheme, and so was Edward Everett Hale. Their influence got him into the White House and into the halls of Congress. Politicians were all willing to help him . . . if someone else would take the responsibility. Mercer haunted the capital for months, but he couldn't find anyone who was willing to sign his name. Finally, as a last resort, he visited General U. S. Grant.

Grant was the hero of the nation and could afford to stick his neck out further than was safe for ordinary congressmen and cabinet officers; more important, he had served in the far Northwest as an unhappy captain with a low efficiency report. He knew that the loneliness out there could drive a man to drink, and had in his case. He was not only sympathetic. He was willing to sign his name to an order providing Mercer with *"a steamship, coaled and manned, with a capacity to carry 500 women from New York to Seattle"*. President Johnson and his cabinet were perfectly willing to back Grant as long as his name, not theirs, appeared on the order.

Mercer, filled with new zeal, *"went out among the people to gather up the women"*. In no time at all he had issued the whole 500 tickets for the voyage. Then he went back to Washington to pick up his steamship. Again fate delivered a knockout blow to the youthful college president from Seattle. He joined the line of claimants who were besieging the desk of quartermaster-General Meigs. The man just ahead of him in line was an unethical individual who, having had a horse confiscated by the army, had already presented two claims to the government and collected on both of them. He was apparently prepared to go on collecting the price of his horse over and over as long as the Federal treasury held out. Unfortunately, however, the choleric General Meigs recognized him this time. He flew into a rage of a magnitude unusual even for a quartermaster-general. In Mercer's own words, *"The quartermaster ordered the man arrested and filled the room with the smoke of vituperation and cuss words until breathing was an actual effort"*.

The general was still black in the face with unexpected rage when poor Mercer timidly proffered his paper, and the general used up the rest of it on the young man from Seattle. "There is no law justifying this order", Meigs huffed, "and I will not honor it". He gave every indication of following this up with an order for Mercer to be thrown in the cell with the erstwhile horse owner, "So", Mercer reported, "crest-fallen, I retired".

General Meigs had the law on his side, but he did cool off after a while and offer to let Mercer have the transport *Continental* without public bidding at the minimum appraisal of $80,000. It might as well have been eighty million as far as Mercer was concerned. He was ready to abandon his dream when a suave gentleman named Ben

Holladay called upon him. Holladay was in the process of building up a West Coast transportation empire and he knew a bargain when he saw one.

"I'll put up the money for the *Continental*", he offered, "and you buy her for me. In return I'll pay all the expenses of the trip out and carry your 500 passengers at a mere token fare". Mercer agreed. There didn't seem to be any alternative. Holladay came back with a pair of high-powered New York lawyers and a copying clerk who was said to be able to write the Lord's Prayer on the head of a pin. The lawyers dictated the contract, the clerk copied it, and Mercer signed it. Not having a magnifying glass, he wasn't aware that the contract was void if less than 500 passengers were embarked for the voyage to the promised land. Even if he had known it wouldn't have bothered him. He was an incurable optimist and he had more willing passengers than tickets.

With the sailing date a few days off, James Gordon Bennett's enterprising New York *Herald* found itself temporarily short of really sensational news. In such cases it was the *Herald's* policy to manufacture some of its own. The Mercer Expedition was a natural. The morning edition appeared with scare headlines that would have done full justice to a verified report that the world was coming to an end. It announced flatly that Mercer was a monstrous practitioner of white slavery who was engaged in luring the flower of Eastern womanhood to fates far, far worse than death in the brothels of profligate Seattle.

By evening the yarn was being copied by papers all up and down the eastern seaboard and pure young ladies were clipping it to put with the tickets they were scornfully mailing back to Mercer. The *Continental's* passenger list had soon dwindled to less than 200, a fact which Mercer explained sadly to Ben Holladay. The magnate got out a magnifying glass then, and showed him the small print. It agreed to carry 500 females at bare cost, but any other number than that would have to pay full fare. It was another blow, but Mercer was in too deep to back out. He agreed, expecting that at last the migration would begin.

The *Continental* stayed in port for months while Holladay had her fitted out to his satisfaction. The passenger list dwindled to a hundred determined young ladies while Mercer's bankroll dwindled to nothing. Various Seattleites had entrusted him with funds for other purposes, but he was a true crusader. After his money was gone he used theirs.

The *Continental* finally got under way in January, 1866. The party had paid first class rates, but they were served the food that had been intended for the cutrate cruise. It consisted mostly of parboiled beans. The girls survived, however, and they felt much better when the ship arrived in the warm ports of South America and was boarded by gallant Latin gentlemen who suggested that they stay there and live in haciendas instead of going on to Puget Sound and log cabins. Mercer was still persuasive despite his many trials, and in due time the *Continental* waddled through the Golden Gate with all the girls on deck and accounted for. There the skipper announced that they had reached the end of the line. The *Continental* wasn't going any further.

Mercer was now stranded in San Francisco, which happily answered to the title of wickedest city in the world. He was in sole charge of a bevy of virginal pioneers with hearty appetites and he had just three dollars to his name. He used it to send a telegram to Governor Pickering of Washington Territory who, he recalled had been one of the most enthusiastic backers of what the jovial politician called "Mercer's raid on the widows and orphans of the East". He also recalled that Pickering had shaken his hand warmly upon his departure for the East and said, "God bless you, Mercer, and make your undertaking a great success. If you get into financial trouble and need money do not hesitate to wire me and I will give you help".

Help was what Mercer needed. *"Arrived here broke"*, his telegram to the governor read. *"Send $2000 quick to get party to Seattle"*.

The governor's response was prompt. There was a collect telegram waiting at the office the next morning, but it would cost $7.50 to take delivery. Mercer explained the situation to the clerk, who decided to gamble a little on behalf of the telegraph company. If the message contained the money order Mercer was expecting they would collect their fee and Mercer had made it clear that there was no hope of payment if it didn't.

Even the telegraph man had to laugh when he read the governor's message. It was a combination of political speech and congratulatory message. It contained well over a hundred words, but not one of them made any mention of money.[4]

Mercer had just one card left in his deck. He had placed orders for goods while he was in the East—some for himself, some for other Seattleites. Most of the merchandise was waiting on San Francisco wharfs for shipment north. It was all in his name, so he had no trouble in selling the whole consignment. That got the girls out of San Francisco in small batches. They travelled the rest of the way to Puget Sound on small lumber brigs and schooners and each arriving group was met with undiminished enthusiasm at Seattle. Most of the girls were married within the year, one of them to Asa Mercer, and the expedition has gone down in history as a great enterprise. The Mercer Girls became the fabled mothers of Seattle and thousands now proudly trace their descent to them.

But poor Asa Mercer was not appreciated until a generation had passed. Most of those who had entrusted business funds to him hadn't intended to be philanthropists. Several of his relatives and best friends were among those who found themselves flat broke as a result of the Mercer Girls' pilgrimage, and many more were badly bruised and bent. The cry of "We was robbed!" resounded from Seattle's seven hills, and it couldn't be drowned out by the strains of the wedding march issuing from Uncle Dan Bagley's White Church.

Asa Mercer, the unappreciated genius who had tried to furnish Seattle with an adequate supply of pure womanhood, was forced to leave town in disgrace to begin a new life as a cattle rancher in Wyoming.

---

[4] In justice to the governor, it should be mentioned that the Territorial treasury was empty and he hadn't been paid for several months himself.

John Pennell's enterprise on the waterfront continued to prosper for a long time after Mercer was gone. His importations had lacked the much publicized purity of Mercer's but they had one big advantage. They hadn't cost the town a dime for travelling expenses. No one ever got around to running Pennell out of town. Even after 1869, when Seattle became a full-fledged town, with a mayor (H. A. Atkins) and a chief of police (John Jordon), there was sin on the sawdust south of Yesler's skid road.

Seattle Sunday Times

s.   SEATTLE, WASHINGTON. DEC. 19, 1909.   FIVE CENTS EVERYWHERE.

Umbrella Man Who Made Seattle Weather Famous

ROBERT W. PATTEN.
The original of "Dok" Hager's cartoons.

PATTEN ONLY BENEFICIARY OF WEATHER

Near-Centenarian, Who Sports Fantastic Umbrella Headgear Discloses Sad Story of Life to The Times.

THREATENS TO LIVE TWENTY YEARS MORE

When It Comes to Knowing "Bill" Seward, "Old Muggs" Stanton and Other Celebrities, He's There.

ROBERT W. PATTEN, the only man on earth that the peculiar climatic conditions of Seattle ever made famous; who says he is about a hundred years old, who wears an umbrella attached to his head, rain or shine, and who has a war record, believes, that would make one E. Bonaparte turn green green with envy, announced a kind tale of woes yesterday afternoon that he was born in New York on February 14, 1812, and that he intended to keep right on living for twenty years yet, that he intended to do such things in Seattle and that he would during the balance of his existence here, wear nothing more on his head than a frame of hair and a miniature umbrella.

There was no particular occasion for Mr. Patten to break forth in permanent gushes yesterday relative to futurities, but he did it just the same, and to tell the truth, as he is accustomed to remark here a score of years and tie such things first, public announcement that he is to pass out of age, his standpoints etc. worthy of some significance. Nevertheless he said that Mr. Patten is the one and only original model for that famous daily living pictures on the weather situation in The Times, which makes Patten the one and only man that that Seattle weather has made famous. Nobody else wants to be, under the circumstances.

Patten Real Warrior.

As the real warrior once Patten had every other fighter absolutely backed off the map. He says so himself. He is the original battle-scar of this country. He fought, he says, in the Mexican War, all the bother ways and had a leading part in the War of the Rebellion. There is no doubt about the latter statement, for Mr. Patten bears a wound that makes his character in the head with a bullet at the battle of Antietam. He was shot eight more times at the same battle, he says, but the bullet that eliminated him for all he says, so safely anchored was the particular pictures

WORKING ON THE RAILROAD

LITTLE VIRGINIA BELL had been an awe-struck child of five at the wedding of Seattle's first lovers, David Denny and Louisa Boren. In 1872 she was a charming young lady of 24, and she was having a wedding of her own.

To Louisa Denny those two weddings—hers and Virginia Bell's—summed up the changes that had come to Seattle in a few brief years. She remembered struggling into her homemade wedding dress in the loft of the windowless cabin David had built for her in the wilderness that had been their claim. She remembered the loneliness and the unbroken forest and the unlighted shore. Hers had been a wilderness wedding. Virginia's was a town wedding.

The wedding party met at the two-story white clapboard house of Carson Boren before moving to square-towered Trinity Church and the bride was lovely in a panniered gown of white silk, brought down from Victoria on the *Eliza Anderson* and sewed by a French dressmaker who had once had her own shop in New York.

Old Mr. Maydenbauer, the town baker, came puffing up with the cupid-bedecked wedding cake clasped tightly in his own pudgy hands, and Uncle Tom Mercer came with a flourish in a brand new red-wheeled express wagon to drive the bride and groom to the church. Afterward there would be a grand reception in the beautiful Occidental Hotel at Pioneer Place.

The horses that drew the bridal wagon were the black mare, Tib, and her stallion mate, the two who had come up out of the sea to give Seattle its first transportation system, and most of the founding fathers were there to watch them draw the bridal party to the church; massive Henry Yesler, whittling on a soft pine stick and Doc Maynard, not quite steady on his feet, but dapper and full of mirth, and Arthur Denny, graying now, and growing portly, but still the beloved father of the town.

The church was crowded and glowing with soft lights and Louisa Denny was sure that civilization had come at last. Afterward she spoke of it to David as they drove back toward their house beyond Belltown, the horse's hoofs falling softly on the leafy road between the tall fir trees and the lights of the town growing small behind them.

"Time passes so quickly when you're busy—and happy", she said softly.

David chuckled. "Busy and happy", he repeated. "You're right, Lou. Seattle's a real town now, which took some doing, and I guess I'll never be as happy as I was when I crawled out of my wet blankets out there at Alki and saw you coming in with the *Exact*".

Louisa Denny could smell the scent of sweetbriar on the night breeze from the Sound and she knew they were nearing home.[1] "Sometimes I can't help wondering how we did it, David", she said wonderingly.

David Denny's broad smile flashed briefly. "It's simple, Lou. Like Arthur says, we did it with muscle and timber".

Muscle and timber had, indeed, given Seattle its start, but it was the coming of a railroad that had made it into a town.

When Governor Stevens arrived to take over his new territory in 1853 it was assumed by Seattle and the whole

---

[1] The Denny farm, deep in the forest, was located at the present site of the Civic Auditorium and the cornerstone of the Auditorium contains a dried sprig of Louisa Denny's sweetbriar—placed there by Historian Clarence Bagley, son of Rev. Daniel Bagley.

Pacific Northwest that the transcontinental railroad would soon follow him to tidewater on Puget Sound. Most of the settlers who chose Seattle for their homes were prompted, at least in part, by the conviction that when the railroad did come it would cross the mountains through Snoqualmie Pass, in Seattle's back yard, and make its terminus on Elliott Bay, which was Seattle's front yard. When, in 1870, the Northern Pacific actually began to lay track across the continent Seattle had its first boom. The population rose from a few hundred to almost two thousand.

It had taken twenty years for the rails to cross the continent and reach Washington Territory and when they did arrive it wasn't by the logical route through Seattle's mountain pass. The Northern Pacific had been granted alternate sections of land 23 miles deep on each side of any right of way it built, so there was no point in trying to save mileage. It didn't escape the attention of Jay Cook, who attained control of the line while it was still building, that a circuitous route by way of Portland, Oregon, would add several million acres of rich timberland to the company's take. That meant that the main line would end at the Columbia River and Puget Sound would get only a connecting branch. But even that was an awful lot better than nothing. Every settlement on Puget Sound began scrambling for the plum; the railroad terminus that would send land values skyrocketing and make up for the years of beans and clams and leaky log cabins in the rain.

On July 14, 1873, Arthur Denny got a telegram from the railroad's commissioners. It came from the company's new town of Kalama and it was short and bitter. *We have located the terminus on Commencement Bay,* the message read.

Commencement Bay was over twenty miles to the south. There wasn't even a town there. At first everybody thought it must be a mistake; then they realized that it was a disaster worse than the Battle of Seattle, and the timid souls reacted as they always had and probably always will. They packed up their belongings and headed up the Sound to safer ground; to the shores of Commencement Bay this time.

The whole thing was like a nightmare to those who were left. It just didn't make sense to them, but it did to Jay Cook and the eastern financiers who were milking the railroad for all it was worth and maybe a bit more. Seattle and Olympia were the established metropoli of Puget Sound. Both towns were claiming that they had passed the 2000 mark in population, which was their downfall in the great railroad lottery. Northern Pacific officials figured there would be a lot more profit in making an entirely new city of their own than in helping to develop an established one where all the choicest claims had already been staked.

Thus was born the city of Tacoma; born with the avowed purpose of putting Seattle out of business and turning Elliott Bay back to the Indians. It was a threat that should have frightened those who stayed in Seattle, for it was backed by irrefutable economic laws and a multi-million dollar corporation, but instead of scaring them it made them mad. The whole town met on the sawdust fill and filed into Yesler's Pavilion to hear fighting words from the founding fathers and from the golden-tongued orator, Selucious Garfielde who had represented Washington Territory in Congress. The outcome was simple and direct; Seattle would build its own railroad across Snoqualmie Pass to the Walla Walla country, where it would tap the golden harvest of Inland Empire wheat, divert it from the hated Northern Pacific, and bring the world's grain fleet to the wharves of Elliott Bay.

The Seattle and Walla Walla Railroad and Transportation Company was organized forthwith, a half million dollars in stock subscribed within two months, and then the town went down to the banks of the Duwamish River to start clearing the right of way with its own hands. There was a lot of eating and drinking and some impassioned speeches first, but when massive old Henry Yesler was called on and responded with, "*Let's quit fooling and get to work*", everybody followed his advice.

It was foolish, of course; a village of 2000 souls . . . less since the timid ones had fled again . . . trying to build a railroad hundreds of miles long across a great mountain range with half a million dollars and their bare hands. But it was the kind of foolishness that captures the imagination.

The railroad corporations were beginning to emit an odor that smelled like scandal to the American public and Seattle's gallant, lopsided fight against them was fine copy. The story spread across the nation. It was a nation that had always taken to an underdog that wouldn't admit he was licked and the name of Seattle came to sound something like a battle cry to independent minded folks back East. Quite a few of them headed West to get in on the fight . . . men whose names were to loom great in Northwest history; men like James Colman, Orange Jacobs, John Leary, Robert Moran, Edmund Meany and Thomas Burke.

The Northern Pacific Line was finished between Kalama and Tacoma in the early autumn, but it didn't come in a blaze of glory. It came limping down to tidewater for a dedication that made Seattle forget its blistered hands and empty pockets while it had a good hearty laugh. At the rate the Seattle and Walla Walla was progressing it was going to take them at least a hundred years to reach the wheat fields on the other side of the mountains and it was pleasant to witness somebody else's discomforture for a change.

Jay Cook's financial empire had come crashing down around his ears in September. The panic of 1873 was ushered in by the clanging shut of the bronze doors of his New York bank. The Northern Pacific was broke, but it dragged into Tacoma on credit and promises. It was raining dismally when the last spike was driven, a plain iron spike. There was no money for a golden one. Tacoma's 200 citizens mustered up a cheer when the first train rolled over the new track, but it was drowned out by the snickers of Seattleites and the angry rumble of track workers who hadn't been paid for weeks and were running out of patience. When no money was forthcoming they proceeded to pile ties across the track for a starter, promising to tear up the rails and carry away a couple of bridges for security if something wasn't done in a hurry.

The dismal ceremony ended with the gentle sobbing of

steam from the marooned locomotive and the loud wails of children who had never before seen a train and had now been denied a ride on this one.

Seattle had reason to laugh, but it couldn't laugh away Tacoma's railroad. It stayed put, linking Commencement Bay with the rest of the United States and leaving Seattle more isolated than it had been before the railroad came. The Northern Pacific got control of the Sound steamboat lines and worked out schedules so that anyone who wanted to get in or out of Seattle had to stay overnight in Tacoma to catch a train or boat.

Seattle's homemade narrow-gauge line was taken over by a canny Scotch engineer named James Colman, who had turned up in Seattle in 1872 to lease Henry Yesler's sawmill. For a while Colman lived in the cabin of a wrecked clipper ship on the waterfront, but when the waterfront fill engulfed the clipper he built the Colman Building above it. A Colman building is still there, marking the grave of a once beautiful ship which lies in the heart of a city.

Colman extended the railroad to the newly discovered coal fields beyond Renton, fifteen miles all told, and the little line did bring a lot of ships to Elliott Bay, although they came for coal and not for wheat as had been originally planned.

Then a man named Henry Villard came to Seattle, and it was a case of love at first sight—on both sides. Villard was a young ex-newspaper man who had come West as a result of the financial crash. Ben Holladay, who played a dirty trick on Seattle by taking over the Mercer Girls' ship and feeding them on boiled beans, was among the fallen giants. He had been financed by German capitalists, who sent Villard out to see if anything could be salvaged. He ended up in control of both Holladay's steamships and Jay Cook's railroad. Seattle couldn't help loving the man.

It became an undying passion when Villard announced that the ruining of Seattle village wasn't essential to his plans; that he was taking over the little railroad to the coal mines, that he was ordering construction of an extension of the Northern Pacific from Tacoma to Seattle, and that he might even dig a canal between Puget Sound and Lake Washington.

Harvey Pike, who had first pick of the university land grants, had bought property where the Montlake Bridge is these days and had proceeded to take the first steps toward making a bridge necessary by connecting the waters of Lake Washington and Lake Union, which were separated by a narrow portage. He did it with a pick, shovel and wheelbarrow, which led Seattleites to feel that a little more digging between Lake Union and the Sound would give them the finest harbor in the world.

Villard was truly winning friends and influencing people in Seattle when he included that long-cherished scheme in the package he was handing them.

Villard came to Seattle to consummate the long-range wooing in September of 1883. He had planned to make his entry in his famous private car over the new spur line from Tacoma, but the line wasn't quite finished. He came by sea, on his liner *Queen of the Pacific*, and every steamboat in the Mosquito Fleet was out in the bay to escort his ship to the dock, where all Seattle was waiting for its hero.

Every building in town, from the coal bunkers, which belonged to Villard now, to the white University building on the hill, was draped with bunting and festooned with evergreens. The hero was escorted under the triumphal arch at the corner of Commercial Street and Yesler's skid road, which was called Mill Street then, to an ornate pavilion on the University campus. Hopeful speeches were made on the plank platform backed by a big painting of the territorial seal with its hopeful motto—*Alki*—which meant by-and-by. Henry Villard couldn't stay for the illumination of the streets that night. He sailed away in the *Queen of the Pacific* and Seattle never saw him again. The greatest love affairs of history have had tragic endings. Henry Villard went broke; stonier broke than Holladay and Cook combined.

The honeymoon was over for Seattle. The Northern Pacific was back in the hands of the enemy. The steamboats went back to the schedules that kept people in Tacoma for 20 hours when they wanted to get in or out of Seattle. Even the 15-mile line to the coal fields was gone. It was a part of the spur line to Tacoma and trains stopped running on that line as soon as Villard crashed.

Seattle didn't hear a locomotive whistle for a solid year, while the unused tracks turned rusty red. Children who had listened to the screeching of attacking Indians instead of lullabys during the Battle of Seattle were grown up by then, and ready for another fight. Among them was Judge Cornelius Hanford, he who had been chased by a very large Indian who had been hiding behind an even larger fir log.

Judge Hanford issued a legal proclamation; the Northern Pacific's Tacoma spur was built on land that had been condemned for public use. Since the company wasn't permitting the public to use it, the farmers along the right of way would be perfectly justified in using the ties for firewood, and in planting potatoes on the right of way. The sturdy farmers took him at his word and began doing just that.

Deeply pained, the Northern Pacific took this orphan line to its bosom again, promising to provide Seattle with railroad service.

The "service" was as much a technicality as Doc Maynard's scraps of paper with "18" scribbled on them in the youthful bride's shoes. Seattle was as little amused as Big Mike Simmons had been by Doc's evasive tactic. Once a day a rusty locomotive ambled down to Seattle pulling a single badly decayed coach behind it. Then it returned, backing all the way, to a place called Stuck Junction, a depressing spot in the woods outside Tacoma. It didn't connect with any other train, it didn't carry freight, and most people claimed they could get to Tacoma faster and more comfortably riding a mule.

But Seattle had other fighters, among them those who had come West because they liked the idea of a frontier village that was willing to take on the financial heavyweights of the nation while building its own railroad with its own hands. One of these was Judge Thomas Burke, who had been studying law in Michigan when he heard about Seattle. Burke was short and stubby. His face was truly the map of Ireland, and he loved a good scrap.

Judge Burke went into cahoots with Colonel Dan Gil-

man, another newcomer who had arrived at about the time
of the honeymoon with Henry Villard in 1883.[2] It was
clear to them that Seattle was hopelessly blocked on three
sides. The Northern Pacific had things sewed up tight to
the south and had blocked the eastern approach to Snoqualmie Pass. The monopoly controlled the Steamer lines to
the west, too, which left only the north; that meant Canada. That way was still open and the Canadian Pacific already had its transcontinental line in operation.

Judge Burke started thumping the drums in Seattle,
while Gilman headed east to look for money. He came
back with enough to build the line across the Snohomish
River. The first division of the new line, the Lake Shore
and Eastern, tapped new coal fields at Issaquah and it began to pay its way. Burke and Gilman were sure that once
they got tracks across the Snohomish they would have no
trouble in raising enough capital to finish the line.

Then the villain struck again. A man from Bellingham
had plans for building a railroad from there to Seattle. He
had little else except a franchise from Congress to bridge
the rivers between Seattle and Bellingham Bay. He claimed
that this gave him a monopoly on all bridge building across
all the rivers north of Seattle. The Northern Pacific backed
him up with enthusiasm and legal talent. The rails of Seattle's second railroad had reached the Snohomish, but eastern investors got wind of the legal battle that was looming
and Gilman couldn't raise any more funds until it was settled.

In Seattle, Judge Burke's legal grapevine informed him
that a Tacoma judge had issued a writ against the building
of the Snohomish bridge; that a lawyer was on his way to
deliver it to the Snohomish County sheriff. Burke hurried

---

[2] Colonel Dan claimed he became a Seattle resident because of a
pair of buckskin pants which he unwisely wore on his arrival in
town in the midst of an autumn rain. "Those buckskins stretched
so when they got wet that the seat drooped down and snagged on
a nail in the sidewalk", he explained. "Then the sun came out and
dried 'em up so tight I couldn't move. By that time I'd decided I
might as well stay permanently."

down to the little Lake Shore and Eastern depot on the waterfront at Columbia Street. A train was due to pull out for Snohomish City in a few minutes. Sure enough, the suspected lawyer was aboard, a suspicious looking brief case under his arm.

Burke found another Lake Shore and Eastern stockholder, John Leary, at the station. They conferred briefly, performed a mystic ceremony over the link and pin coupling between the engine and first car, and then mounted to the locomotive cab.

"*Let her out for all she'll do, and don't stop for anything this side of Snohomish*", the judge ordered the engineer. It was highly irregular, skipping the stops at such important towns as Fremont, Ballard and Issaquah, but Judge Burke was the boss and the engineer would probably have gone along with him anyway. The little judge was the friend of every working man in town, and as a final argument, the little high-stacked locomotive was named the *Thomas Burke*. (The road's other engine was the *A. A. Denny*.) The locomotive headed north at a frightening forty miles an hour, but the two-car train remained at the station along with Tacoma's injunction.

After the locomotive slid to a huffing stop at Snohomish City Judge Burke sent it back to Seattle to pick up the deserted train. Leary went to round up workmen and expedite construction of the bridge. Judge Burke headed for the courthouse for a conference with the Snohomish County sheriff. Snohomish wanted a railroad as much as Seattle, so when Sheriff Whitfield got the word from the judge he gathered up his deputies and departed for the foothills of the Cascade Mountains to, as he put it, look for bandits.

When the train from Seattle finally got in, it disgorged a very angry lawyer with a writ that wouldn't do him a bit of good until he could find someone from the sheriff's office to serve it. It took him so long to locate the sheriff and his deputies that the bridge was finished when he got back. It seemed a little silly then to serve an injunction against building a bridge that was already built and had trains running over it.

It was too much for the Northern Pacific. It bought the

unfinished Lake Shore and Eastern, made a half-hearted
effort to play its old tricks in the way of doubtful service
and high rates, and then gave in completely. When it heard
that Jim Hill was planning to bring his Great Northern into
Seattle the Northern Pacific offered to build a half million
dollar station on the waterfront if the city would just vacate
a few streets west of First Avenue.

This offer caused a grand furor. Everyone had an opinion and most of those who could write sent letters to the
newspapers. It even caused a rift among the old railroad
fighters. Gilman and Judge Hanford were in favor of the
waterfront rail terminal, but Judge Burke sided with those
whose war cry was *"Don't give the Northern Pacific one
damn thing!"* One delegation visited the City Council to
protest that they would no longer be able to fish for tom
cod or dig clams without facing prosecution for trespassing
on railroad property if this outrage were permitted.

Most of the Council had weathered more than one Seattle financial crisis when codfish and clams were the staples
of life and it was said that the stomachs of the town rose and
fell with the tide. They pondered this argument and others,
coming up with a decision not to vacate the required streets
which would have made the downtown waterfront a railroad yard.[3]

Anyway, the important point was this: Seattle had its
transcontinental railroad at long, long last. Four more of
them came to town in later years, but the old-timers never
got the enjoyment from them that they did from whittling
the Northern Pacific down to size. Even today Seattle feels
a little closer to the N. P. than to any of the others.

---

[3] As late as 1923 Judge Hanford viewed their action as a calamity, but few who walk Seattle's stirring waterfront today can possibly agree with the judge on that one.

THE TURBULENT DECADE

SEATTLE WAS ENGAGED in its life and death struggle for railroad service until well into the 1880's, but it was a young and buoyant town with a lot of excess energy left over. It worked off its energy in various directions remote from the big railroad fight . . . in politics, lynchings, building public parks and private mansions, laying streetcar tracks, grading streets and constructing bigger and better brothels to replace the pioneer establishment of John Pennell.

By 1884 the town was claiming a population of "close to ten thousand" and it was still growing while nursing the economic hangover brought on by the sudden puncture of the Villard transportation boom. The Mad House on the waterfront south of the skid road had been replaced by fancier dives of no higher moral character. That section of town had already achieved a reputation which it has never quite lived down. At first people had just referred to it as "down on the sawdust". Now it was called the Lava Bed and, having first been inhabited by a segment of Barbary Coast society, it was following in the footsteps of that notorious district, and at such a rapid pace that Seattle's better element feared it would soon be out in the lead.

The Lava Bed was not only the hangout of what the newspapers called "painted women of the demimonde with the blush of shame long lost and their pink-cuff procurers and panderers", but of out-and-out footpads, strong-arm artists and thugs. A couple of years earlier two of these gentry had strayed from the Lava Bed to waylay a respectable citizen in a respectable section of town. Their victim, a business man named George B. Reynolds, showed fight and was shot. The two habitues of the Lava Bed made off at high speed in the general direction of the waterfront. Reynolds died two hours later. Sheriff Wycoff had been the town's police force for the past twenty years, but most of the solid citizens had suspected for some time that things were getting a little too much for him. They organized a vigilance committee which had hitherto confined itself largely to putting lumps on the heads of outstandingly undesirable residents and then running them out of town.[1]

When word of Reynolds' death was released somebody started banging on the fire alarm. The vigilantes gathered and soon discovered a shoe protruding from under a stack of hay in a waterfront warehouse. The hay stack was surrounded, the shoe removed and found to be on the foot of a likely looking suspect. A little more burrowing brought forth his partner. The crowd thought it would be a good idea to hang them without delay, since the warehouse was equipped with convenient beams and some thoughtful soul had brought along a rope.

The sheriff, however, convinced them that sleeping in a hay stack was hardly a capital offense and they agreed to let him take the pair to jail until more evidence was uncovered. They kept the tell-tale shoe and a little amateur detective work convinced them it was a perfect fit for tracks left in the mud at the scene of the crime.

When the two were taken to Yesler's Hall next morning for a preliminary hearing the place was packed with determined looking citizens, a good many of them carrying the

---

[1] The committee's first recorded activity was the flogging of a pair of Indians convicted of breaking into a store. Carson Boren administered 25 lashes to one, Hillory Butler an equal number to the other. Soon thereafter Arthur Denny reported that similar treatment was accorded the skipper of a sloop who had been selling fire water to the local Indians.

same guns they had used in the Battle of Seattle a generation earlier. Justice of the Peace Sam Coombs was rein-
forced by several armed deputies and the Chief Justice of
the Territorial Supreme Court, Judge Roger Greene, who
had come from a sickbed to help uphold the majesty of the
law.

The prisoners did nothing to endear themselves to the
crowd. They were surly and untalkative. They sounded
guilty even while they were entering their plea of innocent.
As far as the spectators were concerned the culprits had
had their fair trial and now it was time to hang them. The
deputies drew guns, but were quickly disarmed. Somebody
wrapped a tablecloth around Judge Greene's head and
while Justice Coombs was still banging his gavel for order
the prisoners were being dragged down the alley to the corner of First and James. There the crowd removed a couple
of rails from the fence in front of Henry Yesler's house,
stuck them between the forks of two maple trees, tossed
ropes across the rails and strung the two up. They were already kicking at empty air by the time Judge Greene un-
tangled himself from the tablecloth and arrived on the
scene. He tried to cut them down, but the crowd dragged
him away.

As is often the case, love for law and order degenerated
quickly into a lust for blood. The fire bell clanged again
that afternoon and 500 men chipped down the door of City
Hall, dragged out an Englishman named Payne who was
being held on suspicion of an earlier killing, and hoisted
him up beside the other two.

Soon afterward Sheriff Wyckoff dropped dead. The
doctor called it heart failure, but his friends said it was
heart break, which is an entirely different thing. The old
man had seen mob law take over the town where he had
been the law for so many years.

Judge Greene denounced the lynchers bitterly, but few
listened to him. Everyone was sorry about Sheriff Wyckoff,
but they were rather proud of the swift justice that had
been meted out to the murderers. It was in the best tradition of the western frontier. The grand jury refused to issue

any indictments for the participants in Seattle's first major necktie party.

The affair did focus public attention on the Lava Bed district, however, with the result that the municipal election of 1884 was fought out on the basis of a pure Seattle versus a wide-open Seattle. It was the beginning of a trend that was to go on in city elections for close to half a century, making Seattle politics as confusing as a Chinese fire drill to everyone including the candidates for office, who were forced to leap from one side of the fence to the other with alarming rapidity as the wind of popular opinion veered. It was only after state and federal laws robbed the city of much choice in the matter that politicians were reduced to campaigning on such less colorful issues as five cent streetcar fares, economy and that delightfully vague battle cry, "good government".

The 1884 campaign was further enlivened by the fact that the territory's female population had been given the right to vote the year before and the ladies were out to prove that they could bring purity to politics. Many of them were staunch supporters of the People's Party which was using purity as the ammunition to dislodge the Business Men's Party from City Hall. John Leary, the man who had made the locomotive dash to Snohomish with Judge Burke, was the Business Men's candidate for mayor. He was owner of the Seattle *Post*, which hadn't yet joined forces with the *Intelligencer*, and half-owner of the town's waterworks, but People's spokesmen, backed by labor and the feminine contingent, charged that he was "more interested in alcohol than *aqua pura*".

The Business Men argued that times were bad and would get a lot worse if the town went sissified. They pointed to the respectability of their party membership as a guarantee that things wouldn't be allowed to go too far. The purity speakers uttered hollow, ironic laughs as they pointed out that there were plenty of bankers and big dealers behind the Business Men's Party all right . . . Faro bankers and rum dealers.

It was a bitter campaign, with many a Seattle family cleft by a Business Man father and a People's mother, with the children trying to keep out of the line of fire. When it came to a decision at the polls Seattle decided to string along with those who felt that a little sin was preferable to deepening depression. John Leary was elected mayor, to be followed the next year by another representative of business, Henry Yesler. The father of Seattle industry had served a tranquil term in office in 1874, but all hell broke loose this time.

The Chinese had crossed the Pacific to build the railroads. As long as they kept busy at it they were looked upon affectionately by Westerners who wanted the railroads and liked anyone who was willing to build them. But things changed fast after the ceremonial spikes were driven and the bunting was taken down at the new depots. Times were hard. There weren't enough jobs to go around and working men were convinced that low wages were being forced even lower by the competition of ubiquitous "John Chinaman", who was willing to work longer and harder for less pay than anyone else in the world. They were even able to underbid the Indians at their traditional work of picking hops and digging clams. Everyone suddenly seemed to hate the Chinese intensely, goaded on by many newspapers which commented on the problem in the unrestrained journalistic style of the period. In their normal reporting they referred to the Chinese as "leperous, opium-smoking, rat-eating sons of Confucius". When they editorialized they threw restraint to the winds and became downright insulting.

Actual violence broke out first in isolated mining camps and hop fields, where Chinese workers were mobbed and driven out, occasionally with loss of life. Gradually it spread to the cities, where the police generally sided with the anti-Chinese mobs. Tacoma became a center of the movement. The mayor, Jacob Weisbach, was unable to speak much English, but he made it abundantly clear that he was opposed to dirty foreigners who robbed honest Americans of their right to work. The editor of the town's leading newspaper had long been annoyed by the presence of a Chinese garden and laundry next door to his office, claiming that the chattering of its proprietors made it difficult for him to concentrate. He saw his opportunity and helped the mayor fan the flames. The Tacoma Chinese were herded aboard box cars in the rain and shipped out of town.

No violence was done to the deported Chinese, although a few thoughtful citizens felt that considerable had been done to the Constitution and the Bill of Rights.

The Anti-Chinese movement came to Seattle in September of 1885 in the form of a Western Washington Anti-Chinese Congress held at Yesler's Hall. Delegates came from a dozen towns and there were representatives from most of the existing unions. Mayor Weisbach of Tacoma was elected president and a Committee of Fifteen was formed to lead in the projected running out of town of the Chinese population. The mobs had always had full police cooperation in other towns, so it was felt that Sheriff John McGraw should be included in the Committee, but McGraw wasn't available. He was attending another meeting at Frye's Opera House, swearing in new deputies to help protect the Chinese.

Henry Yesler, still hale and hearty at seventy-five, presided at the uptown meeting. He hadn't forgotten the bodies dangling from the fence rails that had been taken from his front yard and he was determined that no more mobs were going to take over his town. The rest of the people at the Opera House agreed with him. It wasn't that they had any great love for the Chinese themselves. In fact it was pretty well agreed that they were going to have to get out, but it was going to be done by due process of law and not with the help of any rabble rouser from, of all places, Tacoma. Furthermore, the Anti-Chinese Congress was serving as a kingsized soapbox for a hoard of radicals and avowed anarchists who were loudly advocating the shooting of bankers and businessmen and the redistribution of property. The bankers and businessmen at the Opera House had mostly started out as mill-hands and lumberjacks and they weren't sympathetic toward the Congress members who wanted to redistribute what they had done a great deal of sweating to build.

The Congress staged torchlight parades and produced

much noise and excitement, but moderation prevailed for a while. Early in November the Opera House Party was invited to meet with the Anti-Chinese Party in an effort to work things out harmoniously. Henry Yesler was asked to preside, and he called on Judge Burke to make the first speech.

The hall echoed with cheering and the stamping of booted feet. Stubby Tom Burke, plain and honest as Irish spuds and always the champion of the underdog and the idol of the working man; he'd see things put straight in a hurry.

But Judge Burke had never straddled a fence in his life and he wasn't in a mood to start then. He was good and mad. His voice cracked like a whip . . . *"He is no true American who will not stand for law and order . . . You have seen in an American city, where a foreigner hardly able to speak the English language holds sway as mayor, a mob in defiance and contempt of law and justice pillage and destroy their business houses and dwelling places and drive them out in midwinter to perish of cold, exposure and hunger"* . . .

Tacoma's mayor knew enough English to understand who the judge was talking about. Hissing and booing filled the hall. Territorial Governor Watson Squire ducked out the back door to telegraph the Secretary of War for Federal troops. Judge Burke had divided the town more neatly than Henry Yesler's headsaw ever split a cedar log.

The party of law and order went back to the Opera House to work out battle strategy. Its roster sounds like the chapter headings of Seattle history . . . Yesler, Leary, Denny, Bagley, Hanford, Lowman, Bailey Gatzert, Haller, Burke, Bell, Frye, Ballard, Minor, Blaine, Carkeek, Kinnear, Dearborn, Meany . . . there were those whose names had figured in that earlier battle that had centered in the same vicinity; Cornelius Hanford, the polite little boy who had escaped a painted warrior to become a dignified judge, and Gardner Kellogg, the fire chief whose stump-blasting cannon ball had belatedly fired the last shot of the Indian War, and the pioneer mother, Louisa Denny, who had rescued her biscuits and her baby from the attacking savages.

They made tough antagonists, and the Anti-Chinese Party was reluctant to tangle with them in a real showdown. Things reached a stalemate when ten companies of infantry arrived from Fort Vancouver in response to Governor Squire's S. O. S. Things were so quiet that they only stayed a week. Fifteen of the Anti-Chinese ringleaders had been indicted for conspiring to deprive the Seattle Chinese of their rights, but no one had been hurt and the charges probably wouldn't be pressed. A lot of the Chinese had already departed—voluntarily and thankfully—and there wasn't anything to worry about except the hard times.

Seattle looked quiet and peaceful enough on the damp Sunday morning of February 7th when the fire bell began hammering again, but Captain Alexander of the steamship *Queen of the Pacific* was worried. The big wooden town with its sawdust streets looked like a perfect fire trap, and he recalled that it wasn't long ago that it had been attacked by Indians. He decided to keep a full head of steam and slack mooring lines. Even when he saw that the town wasn't on fire he had half a mind to pull out into the stream.

The whole population of Seattle seemed to be pouring down Main Street toward the Ocean Dock and the *Queen of the Pacific*, solid masses of humanity jamming the street on both sides and a thin column hedged in between. The Anti-Chinese Party had played it smart; kept under cover until things quieted down and the Army had gone home. Now, with a surprise raid just after dawn they had gathered the Chinese population together to be herded out of town. They were confident that it would all be over before the Opera House Party could muster its forces. They met their first obstacle in the persons of Captain Alexander and his crew, who stood firmly at the foot of the ship's gangplank. The mob had planned on giving the Chinese a free ride out of Seattle and it hadn't occurred to them anyone would be vulgar enough to bring up money matters at a time like that. Captain Alexander was. "What the hell you think I'm running, free excursions?" he roared. "You'll buy a steerage ticket for every Chinaman you put aboard".

The mob was pained at the captain's stuffy attitude and

the failure of the Committee of Fifteen to provide the necessary financing, but the situation didn't stop them for long. Somebody started passing the hat and in a few minutes it was filled with money; enough to buy more than a hundred tickets. One was handed to each Chinese as he was shoved toward the gangplank, but Captain Alexander still wasn't entirely satisfied. He wasn't going to be accused of shanghaing passengers aboard his ship, so he stopped each one to ask, "You want to go to San Francisco?" They all said they did and they seemed to mean it.

Word of the forced exodus was slow in getting to the forces of law and order. The Chief of Police, William Murphy, had been busy helping the mob smash doors in Chinatown and most of the force was helping him. The solid citizens were in church when the alarm came; then the ministers dismissed their congregations and went along with them to get their guns. Judge Greene issued a writ of habeas corpus requiring Captain Alexander to produce all his passengers in court at seven o'clock the following morning. The skipper wished he'd followed his first hunch and escaped from Seattle while the way was clear. It was already past sailing time, his ship was jammed with frightened Chinese and more were crowded on the dock and in the adjoining warehouse. Now he was mixed up with lawyers, which was the worst disaster of all.

Governor Squire read the Riot Act to the mob, but it jeered him and went on hauling Chinese to the dock. The Home Guard Company mobilized at the Columbia Street Fire Station under Captain George Kinnear. They were armed with shotguns and rifles and ammunition requisitioned from the hardware stores. The governor's proclamation was printed and copies were handed out to the rioters, who made vulgar suggestions as to how this legal paper might be used. The Home Guards marched to the waterfront, were jeered, and marched back to the fire station.

Things were nicely balanced. The mob had transported all the Chinese to the ship; the forces of law and order were keeping the ship and its passengers in town by legal injunction. The town settled down to wait out the uneasy night under a downpour of cold February rain. The militia patrolled the streets, but the mob guarded the huddled Chinese on the dock.

Long before dawn the Committee of Fifteen tried another surprise move. Waking a contingent of still non-embarked Chinese, they tied their pigtails together, then marched them in the rain and darkness to the Northern Pacific depot. Seattle's one train a day pulled out at four a.m., and most of the mob went along to enjoy the humor of the situation. They were getting a big shipment out of town under the nose of the law and were playing a delightful trick on Tacoma by dumping a trainload of Chinese there.

The militia foiled them this time, however. Captain Kinnear had gotten wind of the plot and ordered the train out of town ahead of schedule. When the water-soaked mob returned with its water-soaked prisoners to the dock, it was further outraged to find that the militia had taken charge there too.

At daybreak the militia and the sheriff's posse began conducting the Chinese from Ocean Dock to the gingerbread wooden courthouse on Third between Yesler Way and Jefferson Street. It was only four blocks, a fact which the forces of the law looked upon as a blessing. The street was lined all the way with a growing mass of howling Anti-Chinese sympathizers. The mob had grown to several thousand when Judge Greene opened court. Only a few were able to get inside but all of them were able to make themselves heard.

The judge, like Captain Alexander, asked the Chinese if they really wanted to go to San Francisco. Listening to the angry roar of the mob outside they expressed a desire to *"Go like hellee"* to almost anywhere, just so it wasn't Seattle. San Francisco would do nicely. Then they were marched back to the dock to board the *Queen of the Pacific* again. Everything would have been just fine if the ship had been a little bigger. The law allowed her to carry just 169 steerage passengers, and when that many Chinese had been embarked Captain Alexander had the gangplank hauled in. He wasn't figuring on having any more trouble with lawyers if he could help it. That left more than a hundred refugees still on the dock with the next San Francisco steamer not due for almost a week. Sheriff McGraw and Captain Kinnear were just as unhappy about the situation as were the rioters, but they still had the law to uphold. They formed their forces into a double line with the bewildered Chinese between the files and began a grim parade back up Main Street toward Chinatown where their charges would be kept under guard to wait for the next boat.

They got as far as Commercial Street, but from there on the way was blocked solidly. Until then the rioting had been somewhat like the wars the Puget Sound Indians had fought before the coming of the white men—a great deal of noise and confusion with nobody hurt much, but now it was different. The Chinese had been evicted and they were going to stay evicted, regardless of who got hurt.

The sheriff tried to explain that their tickets had been bought and they were only going back to wait for the next boat. It was no use. He couldn't make himself heard above the mob's roar. Led by a bearded young giant in a logger's stagged pants and spiked boots, the rioters pressed in on the militia, trying to disarm the soldiers who began fighting back with the butts of rifles and shotguns.

"Take their rifles. They're afraid to shoot!", the giant was shouting wildly when he was drowned out at last . . . by the roar of a militia rifle. A ragged volley followed, and then the two forces drew apart, appalled at the violence that had been done. Four of the rioters and all of the Chinese lay sprawled in the muddy street, but none of the Chinese were wounded. They were only being cautious. The four rioters were wounded, but only the young logger seriously. He had taken a rifle bullet through the belly at close range and he was dying. After he was dead it was found that he had come up from a Mason County logging camp a few hours before the shooting . . . just to see the excitement.

The mob held the militia at Commercial Street for almost an hour after the volley had been fired, but there was no more violence; only promises to lynch individual members of the law and order faction. Judge Burke was named most frequently.

After a while the militia started toward Chinatown again. They looked as if they might shoot if they had to, but they didn't. The Chinese were delivered to their homes and that was the last that was heard of them in history. The mob had people whom they hated more than the Chinese, so they left those unfortunates to depart on their own initiative or remain in what was left of Chinatown. Most of them went, but those who stayed were not molested.

The Home Guard returned to the courthouse through a crowd of several thousand that ringed the building. There they were met by a constable from the police court who carried a warrant for the arrest of Judge Burke and four other militiamen. The charge was shooting with intent to kill. The constable proposed to take his prisoners through the mob to the police station, but he admitted there was a fair chance they would be lynched before he got them there; especially Judge Burke.

The peppery little judge was ready to go, but he advised the others to stay where they were. "I've taken my stand in support of the law," he explained, "and therefore I'm under greater obligation."

Chief Justice Greene had taken that stand too, but he wasn't going to see it carried to ridiculous extremes. "These men are officers of my court", he told the constable, "and they're not going to be arrested in my presence". The constable retreated to the police station to consult with Chief Murphy while Judge Greene held a conference with Governor Squire, in the course of which he talked the governor into declaring martial law. Civil warrants couldn't be served after that.

Judge Greene read the governor's proclamation to the crowd around the courthouse and this time they listened. The day's events had been sobering. The mob dispersed. The Chinese riots were over.

Who killed the giant logger? That's a question that has never been really answered, although two men thought they did. Sheriff McGraw made both of them promise to keep quiet about their part in the affair, knowing that more talk could easily lead to more killing. As far as the writer knows there is only one man left in Seattle who was there and saw the shooting. He's not talking either. Even after the lapse of seventy years he figures it's a secret that might just as well be kept.

None of the Opera House party members were ever brought to trial for the killing, but most of them had been executed politically, as they were to discover later. The municipal election of 1886 was the last campaign in the war between conservatives of the Opera House and the radicals of Yesler's Hall and it was an all-out victory for the Anti-Chinese, who were back under the banner of the People's Party. They captured every office on the ballot.

Even good, gray Arthur Denny, the founding father who had sounded Elliott Bay with his wife's clothesline, was defeated in the mayoralty race by a political unknown late-comer named William Shoudy. William Murphy, the Police Chief who had joined the rioters, had been forced by Mayor Yesler to resign, but his was an elective job in those days, and he went back into office on the People's landslide.

The bitterness of the Chinese riots lingered for a long time. Judge Burke, the fallen idol of the working men, was defeated in a try for the United States Senate more than two decades afterward on the strength of that carefully preserved hatred.

The radical element waited for the new city administration to redistribute the wealth, but the victorious officials were sobered by responsibility. City government went on about the same as usual, and so did the lusty activities of the Lava Bed. The only noticeable concession to purity was a request from the Mayor's office that bawdy house proprietors hang cheesecloth over the red lights that marked their establishments. This, he explained, would dim them down somewhat and make the town look more respectable.

As for the radicals, they gave up waiting for the revolution to start on signal from City Hall and drifted off to the logging camps and the wheat ranches. The outraged women of Seattle were informed by the Territorial Supreme Court that their enfranchisement had been unconstitutional. (Only Chief Justice Greene, who was unmarried, had dissented.) Their brief hour of political glory over, the ladies retired to the kitchens where their husbands had told them they belonged all along, and the People's Party lost the next election.

Which accounts for all the participants of that hectic period except the *Queen of the Pacific*. With her name shortened to just plain *Queen* she continued to haul passengers and freight between Seattle and the ports of California and Alaska until just before World War II. Then she made her first voyage across the Pacific—to Japan where she was converted into scrap-iron for the imperial munitions factories. Always an innocent victim of mankind's foibles, the poor old *Queen of the Pacific* ended up as shrapnel to be dodged by the descendants of the pioneers who had known her in other violent times.

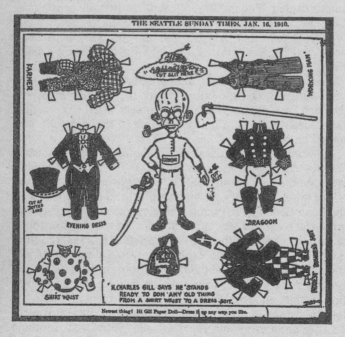

Belevedere Park forms an impressive starting point for a modern-day journey to "Old Seattle."

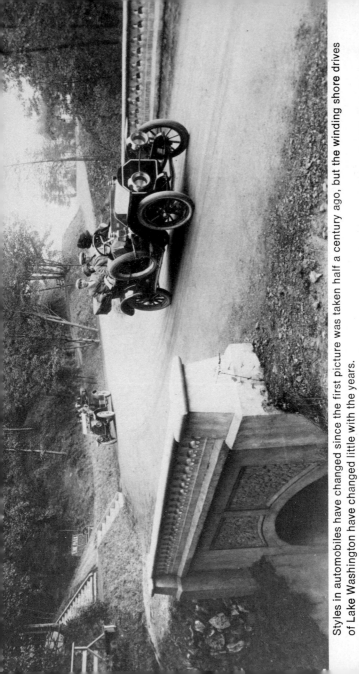

Styles in automobiles have changed since the first picture was taken half a century ago, but the winding shore drives of Lake Washington have changed little with the years.

For the fortunate there may be a glimpse of the *Skagit Chief* or *Skagit Belle*, last of the stern-wheel steamboats, loading cargo for Skagit River landings or making thunderous waterfalls in the harbor with beating paddle-buckets.

Photo by Joe Williamson

Back in the city center, City Hall Park is a vista of green between the 42-story Smith Tower, tallest building in the West
since 1914, and the Frye Hotel. The old stone stairway leads
from the park to Yesler Way, where City Hall workers once
caught the cable cars for the East Side residential districts.

This picture, taken more than forty years ago, the Smith Tower not quite completed yet, shows how few have been the changes of a generation in this, the oldest section of a young city's business district.

Above City Hall Park, redolent of forgotten crimes and the tough, helmeted policemen of other days, stands the old Public Safety Building, unused since a modern 15-story structure replaced it a few years ago.

At Fifth and Denny, a few blocks east of Denny Park, sculptor James Wehn's heroic bronze statue of Chief Seattle stands in surroundings little changed from the November day in 1912 when crowds watching its unveiling blocked traffic on the Queen Anne streetcar line.

Most northerly point of the sentimental journey to Old Seattle is Evergreen-Washelli Memorial Park, also on Aurora Avenue. Here another colorful totem pole stands in the kind of forested quiet which is the totem's proper setting.
Photo by Werner Lenggenhager

TINDER TOWN

THINGS LOOKED GOOD to Seattle in 1889. Most of the decade that was ending had been clouded by the economic hangover that followed the Villard boom and bust, but that was all past now. Congress was getting ready to make Washington Territory a state, a move which was sure to put the northwest corner of America on the map. Seattle, along with the rest of the territory, was ready to forget the most recent bust and start thinking about the next boom. It was predicted that the 90's would be a gay decade.

Seattle was calling itself a city by 1889 . . . a little self-consciously perhaps, but with some justification. There was the population graph which had kept right on crawling up toward the twenty thousand mark all through the hard times and now was almost at that magic figure. There were at least a dozen brick and sandstone business blocks looking more imposing than they really were among the ramshackle wooden buildings that surrounded them. And, proudest boast of all, Seattle had electric trolley cars—scientific wonders which were to be found in only one or two other cities in all America.

There had been horse cars ever since 1884, when Frank Osgood came out from Boston with a bit of capital and a hankering to parlay it into a fortune on the strength of the Villard railroad boom. He stopped off at Seattle for a look around. The actual town didn't impress him much, but the town drawn on paper by optimistic real estate promoters did. If Seattle expanded on the ground at anywhere near the rate it was going on paper a public transportation system was going to be needed in a hurry. There was so much optimism in Villard-happy Seattle that Osgood caught some of it, but he was a true Bostonian. He wasn't going to rush into anything. He went up to Tacoma to have a look at that rival boom town.

When he shook the dust and cinders of the one-car local from his broadcloth prince albert and shiny stovepipe hat at Stuck Junction he found himself surrounded by a group of ardent Tacoma boosters. Ordinarily they ignored the rear-end-first arrival of the train from Seattle, but this was different; word had leaked out that Osgood was looking for a franchise to build a street railway and had cash to back up his plans.

The Tacomans used their stock arguments; building a streetcar line in Seattle, they pointed out, was about as sensible as running one through a cemetery. Seattle was dead and just too stubborn to lie down and admit it.

Their plea was eloquent but it had the opposite of the desired effect. Osgood was surprised to discover that his brief stay on Elliott Bay had made him a patriotic citizen of Seattle. He had a worse case of infectious optimism than he had suspected, and the more he listened to the Tacomans running down his town the madder he got. The love feast at Stuck Junction developed into a heated debate with Osgood using all the arguments of a loyal Seattleite to repel the verbal attack of the hated rivals. He convinced himself, if not the citizens of Tacoma.

Taking the next train back, he promptly organized a street railway company with David Denny and Judge Burke. Within a few months a line of elegant horse cars was operating on Second Avenue from the Occidental Hotel way out north to Pike Street. Within the next two years the line was extended further north to Belltown and north by east from Pike to the forested shores of Lake Union.

This was a far cry from the narrow wagon road the pioneers had hacked to the lake to accommodate Uncle Tom Mercer's team and wagon.

The citizens were so proud of their streetcar line that, when General William Tecumseh Sherman visited their city, they could think of no grander welcome than to conduct him on a horse car ride to Lake Union. The horse cars were a great convenience, but they were limited pretty much to north and south routes. Even Osgood wasn't optimistic enough to expect horses to pull heavy cars up the precipices which passed for east-bound streets above the waterfront. Ezekiel McCausland did provide service of sorts with a horse-drawn omnibus which scaled Madison Street to Boren from a terminus at the corner of First and Main, but only those possessed of both wealth and courage made the trip. The fare was twenty-five cents each way— five times the cost of a horse car ride—and there was always the lurking suspicion that the rig was going to get out of control some day and go catapulating out into the bay.

Cable cars solved that problem. In a few years cables were humming in tune to the jangling bells of little cars which scaled the grades of James, Madison, Yesler and Jackson as capably as mountain goats. A couple of the cable lines pushed clear out to Lake Washington, carrying holiday crowds to picnics and band concerts on the shore and opening up the city to expansion beyond the hilly barrier that had constricted it for so many years. Even the one-time rival town, New York-Alki, renamed West Seattle, had a cable car running from the ferry landing to the hilly residential area above the beach.

In the meantime, Thomas Edison was electrifying the world with his discoveries, among them a demonstration that his strange new force could move wheeled vehicles. Osgood decided to give it a try in 1888, but he ran into opposition at City Hall. The City Council was, in those long ago days, easily frightened by new ideas. The city fathers were all for progress, they said, but Osgood's scheme to run streetcars with electricity looked to them like a science fiction nightmare. They reacted to his request for a new franchise in about the way the present Council might to a suggestion that they solve the transit problem by firing rocket ships from the roof of City Hall to the suburbs.

It was solemnly argued at Council meetings that Osgood's scheme would be a menace to life and limb. Everybody had seen electricity in the form of lightning, and everybody knew that it travelled in a zigzag fashion. How could a car possibly move in a straight line when powered by such an erratic force? It was bound to either zig or zag at the whim of its lightning-like propellent, and heaven help the unlucky people who got in its way when it did.

A Colonel Haines addressed the Honorable Body with this dire prediction: *"Steadiness of movement in the running of cars is essential; electricity is eccentric and shocking. Its shocks will make the cars jump off the tracks and endanger the lives of the passengers. Water is a conductor and rain will divert the electric current from the wires, leaving the cars dead on the tracks or dependent on the efficiency of brakes to hold them from running backward if they happen to be on a grade; collisions and appalling accidents will inevitably occur. The rails will be electrified and horses stepping on them will be shocked and fall".*

Fortunately Seattle's citizens were of sturdy stock, most of the timid souls having already been frightened out of town by Indians, the Northern Pacific and Anti-Chinese rioters. They considered the prospect of having to dodge berserk streetcars and falling horses, but they also thought of the rage and chagrin that would overcome Tacoma when it learned that Seattle was getting something as newfangled as an electric railway. They decided it was worth the risk. The city fathers went along with the tide of popular opinion, granting a franchise to the Seattle Electric Railway and Power Company, which was incorporated on October 8, 1888. In March of 1889 the street railway horses went to pasture. Electricity had taken over.[1]

---

[1] One problem which the street railway critics hadn't anticipated was that of philandering streetcar conductors like Adelbert W. Mudgett of the North Seattle Line. Mudgett had a girl at every car stop, two of whom he actually married—one downtown and one out at the end of the line at Queen Anne town. Things reached a crisis in June of 1892 when both damsels decided to

After that everybody seemed to want to build a streetcar line. David Denny soon had three of them in operation, one running clear to the town of Fremont and beyond to tap the howling wilderness around Green Lake. Judge Burke and William Ballard built a line to Ballard's booming town on the other side of Shilshole Bay, while Osgood started laying track down the Rainier Valley toward Renton. The streetcars made Seattle boom as it never boomed before . . . until the inevitable bust, which came in 1893.

Most of the lines went into receivership then. David Denny, who had once been the whole population of Seattle and was well on his way to becoming one of its first millionaires, lost everything but his shirt.[2] So did a lot of other people. It was symptomatic of a condition that was to afflict the Seattle transit system off and on to the present day.

The resourceful Judge Burke kept his line to Ballard running, but only through heroic economies which included everything but a pay cut for the workingmen who kept the cars running. That he refused to consider. Since he was unable to keep the line's big power house in operation, he closed it up at the suggestion of a young electrician named Sam Shuffleton. The Judge had built a fine brick building on Second Avenue during the era of prosperity, and in its basement was a small electric generator designed to furnish light for the offices and power for the elevators. Shuffleton thought he could make it run the Ballard streetcars too.

He did, surprisingly enough, although the system had its drawbacks. It was a long way from Second and Columbia to Ballard and a lot of current was lost along the way. The cars started out bravely enough, rattling and clanging along

ride conductor Mudgett's car at the same time. It was what Colonel Haines referred to as "an appalling accident" and it took three policemen to get Mudgett safely off to jail.

[2] David Denny never recovered from the financial disaster of 1893. His land claim was still too far north of the business district to be a source of wealth as was his brother Arthur's. He retired to his modest farm with the bitter comment "I'll never look on Seattle again". There he died in 1903. His wife, Louisa, was at his side, as she had been for fifty years.

the downtown streets at a great rate, but toward the end of the line they became enfeebled by lack of juice. You could almost hear them panting, *"I think I can—I think I can—I think I can"*, as they crawled over the last half mile or so of track. Everyone in the Burke Building suffered with them, for the car's struggles dimmed the lights there to a feeble glow while the elevators paused between floors until the trolley made it.[3] But the Ballard Line escaped the fate of the others. It stayed solvent and it kept running after a fashion until Stone and Webster bought the other bankrupt lines and consolidated them into a single system. Then Judge Burke let the big company have his line too.

Horse cars, cable cars and trolleys all operated on a five cent fare throughout their privately owned careers, which lasted for 35 years. After World War I, however, the belief became widespread that public ownership would result in better service and possible lower fares. "From then on", says one historian, "Seattle's transit system has never been out of politics or out of the red".

The five cent fare soon vanished, never to return, and those who rode the city-owned trolleys refused to believe that the service had improved much. By the mid-1930's the ancient orange cars were sway-backed, loose-jointed and gave the impression of being equipped with square wheels. Nobody complained when it was decided to tear up the tracks and replace the sagging streetcars with busses and trackless trolleys. There were few tears shed for the 225 miles of trolley tracks that soon vanished from the city's streets, but it was a different story when the city fathers announced that the eight miles of cable line would have to go.

"The cable lines are slow, outmoded, expensive to operate and they don't reach the present retail center of the city", the experts patiently explained. "We'll replace them

---

[3] This was a convenient thing for hold-up men, who hid in the brush and leaped aboard struggling Ballard streetcars, with such frequency that car men and passengers on that route took to packing guns like the riders of Western stage coaches in cowboy movies.

with super-powered busses that will fairly zip you up the hills".

The public was not impressed. It was recalled that when every other wheel in the city was stopped from turning by the big snow of 1916 the jaunty little cable cars were clanging up and down James and Madison and Yesler Way as dependably as ever they had. Besides, people had a personal liking for them. They were a sort of a tradition. Only two cities in the country still had them.

When officialdom went ahead with plans to tear up the cables citizens formed Keep the Cable Car Societies and fought tooth and nail. The Mayor and City Council had been elected because they said they were in favor of good government; they hadn't said anything about being in favor of doing in the cable cars. Crowds jeered the public officials who proposed such vandalism, but it was to no avail. In 1940 the last little car waggled its tail in a farewell salute to Seattle as it disappeared over the crest of the Madison Street Hill. Then it went out to Georgetown to be cremated along with the 31 other members of its hill-climbing family. The only car to escape the slaughter and remain in town was Old Number 13, which was hiding under a pile of lumber at the power house. It was one of the first, having gone into service in 1888, and now it's the last. You can have a look at Old Number 13 the next time you're out in the vicinity of the Museum of History and Industry.[4]

Although a decade and a half has passed since the sad demise of Seattle's cable cars, those super-powered busses so glibly promised by the experts have not yet materialized, nor has any other foolproof means of scaling the ski-lift

---

[4] The cable cars, like the Sound steamboats, were a link between the old and the new. One Leschi Park car encountered a bear and a cougar on the tracks in the course of one trip to Lake Washington in 1892. On the return trip an aged Nisqually Indian attempted to leave the car while it was still moving. He was badly injured, but refused to be treated by a white medicine man. His tribesmen carried him up the Sound by dugout canoe to be cured by the tribal witch doctor.

streets of the southern business district. The cable cars were sacrificed to progress, but progress has brought nothing to replace them. You can't even ride Ezekiel McCausland's omnibus up to Boren Street nowadays.

The rest of the city as it appeared in 1889 had, like its public transportation system, "just growed" in a Topsylike manner. It had begun with one wooden shack and had multiplied into many, which was fine for a frontier town that had to expand in a hurry, but was hardly in keeping with the dignity of a city. Everybody agreed that something ought to be done about it, but the lopsided frame buildings in the business district were bringing in such fine big rents that the owners just couldn't bring themselves to tear them down.

Henry Yesler and John Leary had joined forces to set an example with the fine three-story Yesler-Leary Building; the town could point with pride to the big Occidental Hotel and Frye's ornate brick opera house, but there was no denying that Seattle was mostly wooden shanties straggling along streets made of planks or a combination of mud and sawdust. Some of the structures were outstandingly ugly even amid their generally depressing surroundings. One was an unpainted frame derelict which sagged disconsolately at the corner now occupied by the seventeen-story Hoge Building. It had been in the line of fire between Indians and defenders during the Battle of Seattle and it still bore the scars of war. Another was Trinity Church just across from the courthouse, which had been the town's pride when Virginia Bell was married there in 1872, and still another was a small wooden building nearby which had once been the village school. It was owned by Henry Yesler and, being convenient to the courthouse, it brought him a tidy rental from lawyers, bail bondsmen and similar legal hangers-on.

It is recorded that one morning when Yesler was passing it while in a mood of violent irritation brought on by the City Council (he was mayor then, and City Councils have always irritated mayors) he met a friend who seemed fascinated by the building's hideous appearance. "Charlie,"

Yesler growled, "if you were just a little meaner I'd give that building to you".

"You must want a powerful mean man to own it, Henry", his friend replied.

"I sure do", said the mayor. "I want the meanest man in town to have it; mean enough to keep it there forever so the City Council will have to see it every time they look out the window!"

Those who have followed Henry Yesler's footsteps in the halls of city government may sympathize with him in the grim revenge he planned against his colleagues of the Council, but fate did not. It had a rebirth in store for Seattle.

It hadn't rained for almost a month, which was something to talk about on Puget Sound.[5] May had been mostly dry and so was the first week of June. The weather was the leading topic of conversation, having taken brief priority over Tacoma's latest act of piracy. The hated rival was trying to steal Seattle's mountain, Rainier, and name it after itself! Outrageous, but the sort of thing to be expected and guarded against when one had undesirable neighbors . . . and the weather was wonderful. The weather was wonderful and Seattle was tinder dry. The calendar on the wall of McGough's paint store and cabinet shop said June 6, 1889. The paint store was in the basement of Mrs. Pontius' wooden building at the corner of First and Madison. Once in a while a cable car clanked by outside, but mostly it was just a quiet, drowsy summer afternoon, with fat flies buzzing around the pot of glue the handy man was heating over a gasoline stove. Just before three o'clock the handy man succumbed to the general drowsiness of the day and let the glue boil over. It caught fire as it dripped onto the turpentine-soaked shavings on

---

[5] It's a peculiarity of Puget Sounders, which has persisted to this day, that they pretend to delight in warmth and sunlight, but are really uncomfortable when the temperature gets much above 70 and things start to dry out. A gentle rain from a soft gray sky is what they *really* like, although few will admit it.

the floor. McGough and the handyman threw a bucket of water on the little fire and it became a big one. They fled then, and none too soon. The Pontius Building flared up like a pitchpine torch.

Seattle had enjoyed the benefits of a volunteer fire department since 1876, although it had gotten off to a bad start. When the first alarm sounded the whole department arrived on the scene in record time, but they had forgotten to take along the fire engine. This problem was solved by the posting of a ten dollar reward for the first team hitched to the engine following an alarm. After that wagons were abandoned all over town when the bell sounded while teams and drivers raced to Widow Plummer's stable, where the engine was kept.

The department had improved considerably since those days and there was no delay in responding to the fire in McGough's shop. The hose cart from Second and Columbia got there first, pulled by a whooping crew of men and boys, but Steam Pumper Number One was a much grander and more reassuring sight when it came rolling in from the main fire station with the big horses' hoofs drumming hard on the dry planked street and the black smoke pouring from the polished brass stack. The hose cart had already coupled onto the fire plug at Madison, so the steamer's crew took the next one, two blocks south. The long dry spell had kept the water level low in the reservoirs. Two feeble streams of water searched for the heart of fire that was hidden in the blinding smoke. An onlooker observed that if someone would treat him to a couple of short beers he could put on a better demonstration than the fire department.

Humorous comment ended when the blaze ate through the walls to touch off the high-proof contents of a liquor store in the Denny Block next door. It spread from there to a row of saloons and in less than twenty minutes the whole block from Madison to Marion was wrapped in fire. The firemen concentrated on trying to keep the flames from spreading to the Commercial Mill behind the Denny Block and to the Opera House and Colman Building on opposite corners of Marion and just across the street from the fire.

The fire bell kept on banging away and Steam Pumper Number Two came dashing up to pump salt water from the bay, but the tide was out; the hose wasn't long enough to reach the heart of the fire.

The crews on First and Marion fought the fire to a standstill for a while, until embers spiralled upward to settle the Opera House roof. Inside of seconds the City's proudest building was roofed with solid flame. Then the whole side of the Colman Building seemed to flare up at once and the Commercial Mill began to burn. The northeast breeze suddenly became a brisk, deadly wind, and the acting fire chief gave way to mild hysterics.[6]

Tough, capable young Mayor Robert Moran took command, ordering the Colman Block and other buildings in the path of the fire dynamited. The flames roared across the wreckage chewing their way south and west across the mill yard to engulf the waterfront docks. Within an hour of the glue pot's tipping it was evident that the whole business district was doomed.

At the courthouse Judge Hanford adjourned the murder trial at which he was presiding. The same sense of propriety which had led him to close doors neatly under Indian attack had kept the legal mill grinding as long as possible, but, like Judge Greene, he wasn't going to carry legality to ridiculous extremes. Besides, the jury wasn't paying attention to business. Some of its members suspected that everything they owned was being burned up by the fire or blown up by the firefighters, and they were right.

Judge Hanford paused at the window to glance at the ugly square bell-tower of Trinity Church silhouetted against the sullen glow of flames. "If it doesn't burn that down the fire's a total loss", he observed dryly. Then he went outside to see about saving the courthouse. Somebody managed to get on the roof and the Judge helped to fill water buckets and hoist them to him by way of the flagpole

---

[6] Chief Gardner Kellogg, after all the false alarms that had been sounded on Seattle's fire bell, was out of town when the real thing happened. He was attending a fire chiefs' convention in San Francisco.

halliards. Dozens of small fires were thus doused on the courthouse roof and that important structure was saved, as was Henry Yesler's grand new mansion across the way where the County-City Building now stands.

The bay stopped the fire on the west after the docks were gone, and it was under control to the east, but there was no stopping its race south to engulf the Lava Bed with its labyrinth of saloons and cheap hotels and fancy bawdy houses on the sawdust flats. It had taken twenty years to develop the Lava Bed from the humble beginnings of John Pennell's Mad House, but twenty minutes of fire wiped it out, which was the end of the Lava Bed for all time. The district itself came back after the fire . . . bigger and gaudier and more sordid than ever . . . but under a new name. People started calling it the Tenderloin after the Great Fire.

Seattle, the lusty young boom-town, had been happily engaged in slugging it out with all the other towns of the Northwest for supremacy and had hated them all cordially; Tacoma most of all, naturally. Seattle, the blasted, burned-out shell of a town found that even ornery neighbors can be mighty comforting to have around when things get really tough. The fire hadn't had much more than an hour's headway when a big red fire engine came rocketing and smoking through town from the waterfront. People cheered through heat-parched throats when they saw the shining gold letters on its side . . . *Tacoma Fire Department.*

A little later the fast steamboat *Fleetwood* came knifing in from Olympia with the foam piled up like surf at her bows and the wood sparks shooting fifty feet in the air from her stack and the capitol city's new steam pumper lashed on the forward deck.[7]

---

[7] Olympia probably hadn't been thinking of a reward when it came to helping out a neighbor, but the bread cast on the waters that day paid off handsomely. Eastern Washington legislators ganged up the following year to take the capitol away from Olympia. It was a well organized plot, but Seattle came to the rescue, on the sound principle that one good turn deserves another. The King County delegation tipped the scales in favor of Olympia.

Strange fire engines kept coming in all afternoon and evening, from Port Townsend and Snohomish and New Whatcom. At half past two in the morning the gleaming pumper *Multnomah,* pride of the Portland Fire Department, came in from Oregon by train, and at four o'clock the side-wheeler *T. J. Potter* came in from Canada with an engine manned by the chief and 22 men of the Victoria Fire Department. Flames were licking at the Canadian Pacific pier and so they stood and fought the fire where they landed.

The fire burned itself out before dawn. There wasn't anything left in the business district or the Lava Bed for it to feed on. The waterfront was swept clean of docks and mills and coal bunkers from Jackson Street to Union. Twenty-five blocks, sixty square acres of the little city had been wiped out overnight. It has been said that the heart of Seattle was destroyed in the Great Fire of 1889, but that's a misstatement.

Tacoma was busy setting up big tents in which to serve 3000 meals a day and the Mosquito Fleet was coming in the bay from all the towns on Puget Sound bringing food and clothing and medical supplies when the sun came up. Then there were signs that Seattle's heart was still beating. Newsboys hit the unburned streets hawking the morning edition of the *Post-Intelligencer* announcing that there had been a fire. The newspaper plant was in ashes, as was that of the *Times,* but a couple of little job presses had been rescued and they were doing their duty. Then a red and yellow cable car nosed over the crest of Madison Street and felt its way cautiously downgrade to where the tracks were warped by the heat of the fire. Word was passed that a meeting was being called to discuss the rebuilding of the town. It was to be held in the armory, which was the biggest building to escape the fire, and the public was invited. Clearly, Seattle, however singed and shocked, was still a city with a healthy pulse-beat.

Historians have made much of an intangible force called "the Seattle Spirit", although none of them have explained just what it is—or was. Popular opinion seems to hold that it's the frame of mind that didn't permit the town to realize that it was licked even when it was apparent to everyone else that it was down for the long count.

What happened at the meeting in the armory while the embers were still cooling probably sums it up as well as anything. After it was settled that the city would be rebuilt of brick and stone instead of wood and sawdust, Mayor Moran brought up the Johnstown Flood, which seemed out of place in a town that had just been destroyed because there wasn't enough water. The Mayor reminded the meeting that Seattle had raised a sizable relief fund to aid the Johnstown Flood victims. It hadn't been sent yet, and in view of their own sad plight they might want to keep it with the justification that charity begins at home.

Seattle voted unanimously to send relief to Johnstown!

SEATTLE 241,500
TACOMA GETS 82,972
CITY OF DESTINY CAUGHT TRYING
TO ADD 33,296 NAMES TO ROLLS

BONANZA

SEATTLE ENTERED a promising new decade, the 1890's, still badly scorched around the edges, but healing fast. Some businesses were still operating from tents, both north and south of Yesler Way, the old skid road, but the new city of brick and stone was rising fast. Guy Phinney's two-story brick on First Avenue was open for tenants four months after the fire. Before midwinter Dexter Horton had doubled the ante with a four-story office building at Third and Cherry. The imposing Pioneer Building, at Pioneer Place, had been under construction when the fire struck. Hot ashes were shoveled out of the excavation and by 1890 the six-story Pioneer Building was topping the city's new skyline.

The respectable part of town was determined to rebuild itself in as nearly fire-proof style as possible, but the Tenderloin was willing to compromise. Sin was for sale under wood and tarpaper roofs long before the banks and grocery stores were able to fold their tents and move to their handsome new brick homes.

Before long the rest of the city decided to follow the example of the Tenderloin and do a little compromising of its own . . . on a purely temporary basis. Nobody had time to count heads, except for a quick roll call which indicated no lives had been lost in the fire, but it seemed as if things were getting crowded. Seattle in ruins appeared to have a lot more people than it had before the fire. It just wasn't possible to build permanent buildings fast enough to take care of everyone. To help solve the problem the city joined forces to build a huge, rambling wooden hotel covering the entire block between Fifth and Sixth Avenues and Columbia and Marion Streets. It had paid for itself by the time fancy new hotels like the Butler and New Occidental were finished; then, true to its promise to itself, the city tore the makeshift down.

When the 1890 census was completed it confirmed Seattle's suspicion that it was having growing pains. Less than a year after its destruction the city had more than doubled its population . . . to 42,837. That was *eleven times* the official figures of the last federal census, in 1880.

Washington had become a state too, during the fever of rebuilding. Ex-Governor Squire, who had called in the Army to end the Chinese riots, was a United States Senator. Judge Hanford, last territorial Chief Justice, was appointed United States District Judge for the new State of Washington. Sheriff McGraw was mentioned as a coming man in state politics, a prophesy which was soon fulfilled. He followed Elisha P. Ferry to the capitol as second Governor of Washington State.

City politics didn't take a back seat to state level statesmanship; on the contrary it became more weird and wondrous than ever. With Washington accorded the dignity of statehood, Seattle was entitled to the corresponding dignity of government by freeholders' charter, a right which it speedily claimed. A new Committee of Fifteen labored for seven weeks under the chairmanship of Judge Orange Jacobs. This painful period of legal gestation brought forth Seattle's first city charter. The baby was accepted by the voters, but not for long.

Apparently determined that the legislative branch of city government was not to become subservient to the executive, the framers of this remarkable document placed city affairs in the hands of a sort of city legislature composed of two houses. The Senate was a board of ten aldermen, while no less than sixteen councilmen composed a sort of poor man's House of Representatives. Without going into the horrible details it is sufficient to say that this unwieldy body was frequently unable to agree on even such basic issues as the time of day.

A few years later the overcrowding at City Hall was reduced somewhat by a reduction in force. A single City Council of thirteen members was provided for in a new charter. The public agreed that this was plenty, soundly defeating a later move to boost the ante back up to an all-time high of thirty city councilmen and a city manager.

In spite of its excess weight, the city government puffed along bravely in an effort to keep up with private enterprise in the race to rebuild Seattle. The city bought property at the worst of the job created by the failure of Doc Maynard's plat to fit the others and fixed things up considerably by widening Front Street and Commercial Street and joining them together to form First Avenue and First Avenue South. Yesler Way, which had first been the skid road and then Mill Street, was regraded to make it match up with the improved thoroughfare. If nothing else it made travel from the respectable part of town to the Tenderloin much more comfortable.

A number of the main streets were widened from 66 feet to 90 feet, a blessing for which the motorists of today would do well to give thanks to that cumbersome municipal legislature of half a century ago. Traffic was a problem even then; the iron tires of drags and wagons busy rebuilding a city were churning the widened streets into muddy rivers. As fast as the rebuilt sawmills could turn out fir planks they were hauled uptown to provide temporary paving for the streets.

New sidewalks were built on the theory that pedestrians should be able to step from them to the street without using ladders, a condition that had not always prevailed before the fire. The sidewalk on the north corner of Second and James, for instance, was two feet lower than the street, while across the way pedestrians could spit tobacco juice into open carriages on the street from an eminence five feet above it.[1] Steps were provided for getting down to street level from the south side of James Street. This was a fine thing for native sons and daughters who knew their way around, but strangers in town sometimes tried to jaywalk in the dark. It was a distressing experience.

That particular state of affairs had resulted from Henry Yesler's determination to have dry cellars under his property, come hell or high water. His house was on the north side of the street with the doorstep two feet below the street grade. He was damned if he was going to have any johnny-come-latelies building sidewalks that would drain into his front door. Similarly, the brand-new Yesler-Leary Building stood five feet above the newly graded street on the opposite corner. It was Seattle's finest business structure and it was obviously more important to get people in its front door than across the street. On that side the walk stayed high.

The fire had solved this thorny problem along with a lot of others.

Three new brick schoolhouses were built to feed students to the white-columned University on the hill, which had escaped the fire. The volunteer fire companies gave way to a full-time paid department, complete with a fire boat, the *Snoqualmie*, which was the first on the Pacific Coast, and the city bought out the Spring Hill Water Company which pumped water from Lake Washington to a big reservoir on top of Beacon Hill. Improvements were planned, not to enhance the potability of the lake water, Lake Washington not then having become the attractive cesspool which it is today, but to improve the pressure at the fire plugs.

All went smoothly until the city, having repaired the worst of the fire's ravages, took time out for a look at the enterprising district south of Yesler Way. The rest of Seattle had staged a remarkable comeback, but the Tenderloin was out in front of everybody. It had, at last, surpassed its

---

[1] and frequently did.

parent San Francisco's Barbary Coast. A lot of nationwide attention had been focused on Seattle as it rebuilt itself and, journalists being what they are, most of the reporters were especially fascinated by the resurgence of the Tenderloin. They informed a shocked nation that Seattle, not San Francisco, was now the wickedest city in America.

Seattle was shocked right along with the rest of the country. The town was wide open, sure, but what Western town wasn't? A little sin was good for business, but this was too much of a good thing. The *Post Intelligencer,* owned and edited then by Leigh S. J. Hunt, snatched up the neglected banner of purity and began to wave it violently on the theory that a well publicized display of virtue would save Seattle's civic reputation.

Hunt summoned the Mayor to his office in much the same manner that he might have sent for a boy from the O. K. Messenger Service. Mayor Harry White, who had succeeded Robert Moran as the first chief executive under the freeholders' charter, was noted for a handlebar mustache so luxuriant that his critics claimed it was sapping his vitality. It did, however, serve to distract attention from a not very firm chin.

Editor Hunt tossed a handful of defamatory clippings dealing with Seattle sin in front of the Mayor. "What are you *doing* about this, Harry?", he demanded.

The Mayor admitted that he hadn't done much of anything, but suggested feebly that nobody had seemed to want him to until now.

Hunt shook his head sadly. "You're on the way out, Harry", he said. "You can do it the easy way by writing out your resignation and leaving it with me, but one way or another you're going". Mayor White wrote his resignation on a piece of *Post Intelligencer* stationery and it was duly printed in the next morning's edition.

Editor Hunt had achieved both a journalistic scoop and a new city administration with a minimum of effort. George Hall, President of the Board of Aldermen, filled out White's unexpired term, to be followed in 1892 by James T. Ronald, who led a full slate of purity candidates into City Hall. Like many advocates of good government before and since, Seattle's crusaders discovered early in the campaign that a little mutual horse-trading was essential to political success, however pure the motives of the campaigners.

Choice plums on the purity ticket were awarded to representatives of the city's most influential racial groups . . . the Irish could name the Police Chief, the Norwegians the Harbormaster, and so on. The practical Germans chose the office of city treasurer, with the result that a popular baker named Adolf Krug was selected for that important job.

Krug's success in the bakery business was based on his reputation for having an accommodating nature, a trait which he carried with him to City Hall. The city was rebuilding itself so fast that it had used up all the cash in the till and was operating on credit in the form of treasurer's warrants, which couldn't be cashed but paid liberal interest to their holders. Treasurer Krug had prosperous friends with money to invest who were willing to buy city warrants at a discount as fast as he could stamp them "Unpaid for lack of funds". On the other hand, he had many less prosperous friends who needed cash loans. The ingenious baker hit upon a plan to satisfy both groups. When the treasury took in a sack of cash he loaned it to his needy friends, thus permitting him to issue more warrants to be sold to his prosperous friends.

Krug thought he was keeping everybody happy until the City Council discovered what was going on. Then all hell broke loose. Poor Krug, who hadn't meant any harm, took fright and bolted. He was tracked down and sent to prison and most of the warrant buyers and borrowers were also arrested, although never brought to trial.

When a deputy sheriff went with a superior court bench warrant to arrest one of the prosperous element in that Teutonic version of frenzied finance he was refused admittance to the owner's substantial home on Capitol Hill. "Open up!", he demanded, "I'm from the courthouse and I've got a warrant for you".

This enterprising investor had been reading the papers and he knew what was going on. Outraged, he bellowed through the closed door, "Go to hell mitt your varrant! I am not buying any more varrants!"

The reform party thus provided Seattle with a belly laugh which was cherished for many years, but it accomplished little or nothing of its avowed purpose to clean up the Tenderloin. A few of the more notorious dives were padlocked, but the horrifying discovery was then made that such treatment simply spread the disease without curing it. The former denizens of the padlocked premises just moved into respectable neighborhoods and carried on business as usual. It became necessary to caution servants in even the best districts against addressing their lady employers as "madam". There were so many of the real thing around that it was no longer a respectable title.

Seattle had found a logical argument for keeping hands off the district south of Yesler Way: "If you don't allow a restricted district you'll have pimps, pickpockets and prostitutes moving in next door to you in the decent parts of town". It was an argument that made sense to a lot of people for a long time.

But the advocates of one hundred percent civic purity didn't give up the fight immediately. In 1894 they elected Byron Phelps mayor and also achieved a majority in the City Council. Then they set out to break the backbone of the Tenderloin—the box houses.

These interesting establishments combined the more desirable features of saloons, burlesque theaters, dance halls and brothels and, from the standpoint of their proprietors, they were highly profitable. Most of them, like the Comique which is still remembered nostalgically by many a solid citizen of mature years, were located in cellars below street level. They were equipped with a long bar, a stage and runway and a bevy of girls in paint and tights. From time to time the girls would appear on stage to bawl a song or prance through a bump and grind number, but mostly they circulated through the room and into the curtained boxes at the rear which gave the places their name and a good deal of their popularity.

The girls' ostensible source of income was from the promotion of bar sales. A pair of beers or a round of whiskey were accompanied by metal checks which were good for a cash commission at the close of business. A bottle of wine netted a dollar profit for the hostess and a magnum of champagne was worth two dollars. Most of the big spenders frequented the boxes, which were luxuriously appointed, even to comfortable sofas from which the customer could watch the stage, if he so desired, and order drinks from the bar by punching an electric button.

The girls were allowed to follow the dictates of their consciences as to just how far they should go in boosting liquor sales, but all the giggles and girlish shrieks which emanated from the curtained boxes didn't come from them. Ladies of the street circulated freely through the house and into the boxes, competing with the regular employees for the bankrolls of the customers.

A fair percentage of the box house girls were, contrary to popular legend, highly respectable young ladies who preferred what the reform element called "the wages of sin" to the starvation wages paid—frequently by those same reformers—to shop girls and office girls in the respectable sections of town. Box occupants had no difficulty in picking these properly brought up maidens from their fallen sisters. If, after making an immoral suggestion, the occupant received a stunning blow on the head he knew that he was drinking with a nice girl.

The research which makes possible such detailed information was done at the Comique many years ago by an observer in whom this writer has the utmost confidence. As a matter of fact it was this writer's father.[2] Dad always makes it plain that he wasn't there because he wanted to be. He was working his way through the University of Washington and one of his jobs was that of bodyguard to a Tenderloin gambler. The gambler needed a bodyguard because he had sold a number of building lots on Green Lake to some of the more affluent prostitutes of his acquaintance. When the girls got out to Green Lake and discovered

---

[2] Roy E. Newell, author of the unpublished manuscript, "From Buffalo Chips to Blue Chips".

that their lots were miles from nowhere and covered with —of all things—virgin timber, they vowed to cut out the liver and lights of the gambler with dull knives.

Their threats made the gambler nervous, but he loved the Comique and went there almost every night. Dad, of course, had to go with him, and of course he couldn't help noticing the girls in tights; there were so many of them. During the day he had another job—a college education didn't come cheap even in those days. He drove a laundry wagon around the northeast part of town and a number of his customers were prim, proper ladies in shirtwaists and pompadours . . . who spent their nights earning an honest buck at the Comique and the other box houses down below the deadline.

Mayor Phelps delivered a body blow to the box houses, however, and the gaiety south of Yesler Way came to a screeching halt . . . for a while. A city ordinance was passed making it illegal to sell liquor in a theater and Phelps cops enforced it to the hilt. The box houses couldn't survive on a temperance basis. They were something you had to be good and drunk to appreciate. One after another they closed their dingy doors and the city's leading box house proprietor, John Considine, departed to try new ventures in Spokane. Even the Tenderloin became subdued for a little while.

Jim Hill had brought a transcontinental railway—the Great Northern—to Seattle, but the Panic of 1893 came with it. It hit Seattle later than it did the East, but it hit harder. The dozen independent streetcar lines went into receivership. So did the Northern Pacific and the Oregon Improvement Company which owned the coal mines behind Seattle and the coal bunkers on the waterfront. Founding fathers like David Denny, who had grown big and wealthy with their city, found that they were right back where they had started, except that they weren't young any more. The tides of Puget Sound were dictating to people's stomachs again as the city fished for tom cod from the docks that were lined with idle ships, dug clams on the tideflats and waited hopefully for better times.

They waited four bitter years, through times so tough

that the fire department couldn't buy hoses for the beautiful new engines that had been bought after the Great Fire and even suffered the indignity of being required by the City Council to use the proud fire boat *Snoqualmie* to tow the city garbage scow; through an ever-worsening depression that saw some of the new brick schools closed because there was no money to pay teachers.

The Depression was at its worst by midsummer of 1897. To add to the mood, forest fires were raging unchecked as they did every summer throughout the Northwest. It was twilight at high noon and eyes burned from the acrid smoke that filled the air. Clouds of insects, driven out of the woods by the fires, settled on the town. More than a hundred families—practically all that could afford tickets on the West Seattle Ferry, were camping out at Alki Point where sea breezes made things a little more pleasant.

Out at the foot of Magnolia Bluff the Army was staking the ground for a new military post, Fort Lawton, which people hoped would bring a little money into town, but there wasn't much else to be optimistic about. Edwin R. Lang, billed as Seattle's favorite comedian, and his trained dog, Schneider, were costarring at the Seattle Theater in "Rip Van Winkle", but most folks had to compromise on the *Post-Intelligencer's* free concerts in the park, which featured Dad Wagner's Military Band.

If you had the money you could buy a seven-course French dinner with wine for 50¢ at Ike Rosenthal's Royal Cafe, an elegant wool Chevoit suit for $3.90 at the Bon Marche, a comfortable rocking chair for $1.85 at the Standard Furniture Company, or three seven-room houses at 9th and Jefferson for a total price of $6000 through Crawford and Conover's real estate office. Lowman and Hanford at Pioneer Place were selling croquet sets at a big discount, while Frederick, Nelson and Munro had just reduced prices "several notches" on all furniture, carpets and household goods.

Few people had the money to take advantage of these bargains. Sometimes Craine's Employment Agency at First and Washington put out a placard for a logging camp blacksmith at $2.25 a day or a teamster at $30 a month and board, but there were twenty hungry men for every job.

Few of them even had much hope, after four years of frustration and poverty. Certainly there was little interest in the strange, brightly lighted balloon-shaped objects which people kept reporting, zipping through the sky at astounding speeds above lower Puget Sound and British Columbia points; not even enough interest to give them a name, so it was another half century or so before they became "flying saucers".[3]

True, a few determined souls had struck out for Alaska, where it was rumored a man could make good wages panning gold, if he was lucky enough to strike the right creek, but Alaska was a long way off. In Seattle, as all over America, times were mighty bad.

The depression was blacker than the smoke-shrouded skies above the town, but when it ended it ended with a whoop and a roar!

The roar had its beginning in the hoarse whistle-blast of the North American Trading and Transportation Company's steamer *Portland* heading in toward Schwabacher's Wharf on the morning of July 17, 1897. The *Portland,* in from the mouth of the Yukon River, had a ton, more or less, of raw Alaska gold aboard.

Tradition has it that the arrival of the *Portland,* which set off the great Alaska Gold Rush, was a completely unexpected stroke of vast good fortune. That makes the story somewhat more dramatic, but it isn't strictly true. Reports of a great gold strike in the Klondike had been filtering into Seattle for months before the *Portland's* historic arrival and the *Eureka* had arrived at San Francisco, treasure-laden, several days before the Portland reached Seattle. Newspapermen were cruising the waters around Cape Flattery

---

[3] The same phenomena were reported from Olympia to Nome in 1908. The *Times* referred to them as "strange lights flashing out of the midnight sky, seemingly supernatural in origin", adding the interesting conjecture that they might have something to do with an effort by residents of Mars to get into communication with Earth. Who says history doesn't repeat itself?

waiting for her and telegraphing regular reports from Port Townsend. Everyone knew the *Portland* was coming with a lot of gold on board, but it took people a while to realize just what her coming was going to mean to the depression-ridden city. The *Times* editorialized dolefully that Seattle would probably suffer a drop in population, since everyone would be leaving to get rich on the banks of the Yukon.

One man who did realize what it could mean was Erastus Brainerd, journalist. A journalist is said to be a newspaperman who is out of a job and that was Erastus Brainerd. He had once edited the *Times* and he had worked for the *Post-Intelligencer,* but when he heard about the *Portland* and her golden cargo he fast-talked himself into a job as press agent for the Seattle Chamber of Commerce.

If ever the press agents of Seattle decide to erect a statue in the park it should be a statue of Erastus Brainerd. He gave the great Alaska Gold Rush to Seattle.

Brainerd was no fly-by-night publicity man, even though his cuffs may have been getting a little frayed by the time the *Portland* put in an appearance. In the East he had served on the staff of the Boston Art Museum, written a book on the fine arts and held top editorial jobs on famous newspapers. As a crowning mark of respectability he was a pillar of the Republican Party. As a matter of fact, Brainerd was a bit *too* intellectual for a frontier newspaperman. People had a distressing habit of falling asleep over the *Times,* or *Press-Times* as it was known then, while Brainerd was its editor. The paper lost money steadily and Brainerd switched from journalism to politics, serving as state land commissioner under Governor John McGraw.

McGraw and Brainerd both lost their jobs in the Populist landslide of 1896. The ex-governor booked passage on the *Portland* for her return trip to the gold fields; the ex-land commissioner set about making Alaska a suburb of Seattle.

The odds were heavily against him at first. The *Eureka* had, in cold fact, brought twice as much gold to San Francisco as the *Portland* had brought to Seattle. The nation had already heard of the million dollar's worth of treasure landed at the Golden Gate and the *Portland* had only brought down half a million.

Brainerd went into a huddle with Beriah Brown, Jr., second generation *Post-Intelligencer* headliner (his father had been one of its first editors) and they came up with a phrase that was to electrify the nation . . . *a ton of gold!*

Even in 1897, newspaper readers were fairly used to reading about millions, so they weren't unduly impressed by the San Francisco dispatches, but *a ton of gold!* That was something altogether different and exciting.

In big black type it swept the nation . . . *a ton of gold at Seattle!* Nobody knew what a million of anything looked like, but everybody could visualize a ton, and visualizing a ton of gold was a real pleasure.

People read the headlines and heard the roar of excitement in drab, depression-haunted towns all over America. The ton of gold had come to Seattle and that was where they were going. Thousands headed for Seattle and Brainerd kept them coming on a storm of news releases datelined Seattle. These were followed up with full-page advertisements in all the important national magazines. Brainerd wrote magazine articles on the Gold Rush, then quoted the articles in more news releases. Booklets and brochures poured from Seattle printing presses. Deluxe editions went to presidents and kings and a hundred thousand copies of the *Post-Intelligencer's* Klondike edition were mailed to public officials and public libraries all over the nation. Occasionally a feeble wail of protest was heard from San Francisco or Portland or Tacoma, but was quickly snowed under by more messages from Erastus Brainerd.

The crowds thickened on the Seattle road. The gold was all in the dispatches from Seattle, so where else would a sensible man go to get some of it? For the first and possibly the last time in history, Seattle had out-balleyhooed California and it was paying off. The depression was over for Seattle. The city swelled and roared with teeming life as every train and steamer poured out its horde of miners and school teachers, ministers and farm hands, gamblers and prostitutes who had come to Seattle to get rich.

Schools were quickly established to teach dog-team driving and the hopeful students went mushing over city streets. Family pooches who strayed away from their own back yards were likely to find themselves in harness and suddenly working for a living. A number of unfortunate poodles, fox terriers and other eminently unsuited breeds were sold as "genuine Alaska sled dogs" to sail north with treasure-seekers whose hopefulness was only exceeded by their gullibility.

Alaska outfitters built walls of goods along First Avenue and as fast as they were built they were torn down by eager buyers. An enterprising inventor ran front page advertisements in the daily papers depicting, in horrifying drawings, the fate of prospectors who went north without an adequate supply of his superior crystalized eggs. The gruesome remains of those not supplied with crystalized eggs lay embedded in snow banks while plump, smiling customers of the egg man pressed on toward a glittering goal of unlimited wealth and abundant health. Even the hens of Seattle strained every fiber to meet the demands of the great Alaska Gold Rush.

Buildings unfinished since 1893, were completed with a rush, and every hulk along the waterfront was pasted together with paint, putty and good intentions to be advertised as a "fast and commodious steamship for the gold fields". Prospective passengers fought to buy tickets and get aboard these floating coffins. Even the ancient *Eliza Anderson* was hauled off the mudflat where she had been dozing for years to try the long jaunt north. She was one of the considerable number that didn't make it.

Up at City Hall, politicians were scrambling to keep pace with the changing times. A hardware merchant named Frank Black had been elected mayor in 1896, but he was not a dynamic leader, nor was he adept at the art of politics. One of his critics had observed that he knew the subject from A to B. Staying in office only long enough for a bewildered look around, Black resigned. The City Council appointed Colonel W. D. Wood to fill out the term.

Wood, a more aggressive type than Black, took over with a firm hand. The lid that had been clamped on the Tenderloin by Byron Phelps was kept on tight by Mayor

Wood, who was well embarked on a genuine civic cleanup
when the Gold Rush started. Then he bought a steamer
named the *Humboldt,* stocked it with trade goods and sold
a lot of tickets for the Yukon. He reserved the very first
ticket for himself.

His Honor not only deserted the city, but committed the
even more grievous sin of buying all his ship's supplies in
San Francisco. He even antagonized the *Humboldt's* passengers, being in such a hurry to start cashing in on the
Gold Rush that he loaded his own freight aboard and then
started to sail away while much of the passengers' baggage
was still on the dock. This resulted in a small-scale riot on
the waterfront, but things were in such a turmoil there by
that time that only an all-out revolution would have attracted much attention.

Most of the Seattle police force went north, too, but they
weren't missed. People were too busy making up for those
four long lean years of depression. The shortage of cops
was noted with approval by some, among them John Considine, the box house king, who was back in town and
strolling the streets south of Yesler Way.

He was looking for a good cellar location.

JOHN CONSIDINE found that cellars south of Yesler Way weren't easy to come by in Gold Rush Seattle. The golden magnet was exerting a strong attraction on gentlemen of a professionally sporting disposition. They were arriving in Seattle on every train and boat—gamblers, saloon men, variety theater operators and brothel-keepers—all intent on garnering their share of Alaska nuggets the easy way. Even the ancient "White Church", where Uncle Dan Bagley had once preached the word of God, its walls still scarred with Indian bullets, was purchased by a syndicate and reopened as a gambling hall.

Considine couldn't find a single unoccupied site that suited him, but he did discover an old competitor of his, the People's Theater operating full blast in a newly renovated basement which he suspected might be occupied on a "gentleman's agreement" basis with the building's out-of-town owner. He followed up his hunch, which proved correct, and was successful in leasing the premises out from under the People's Theater operators.

The jubilant Considine staged a grand re-opening of the People's to celebrate his return to the Tenderloin box house field. The original Little Egypt, the foremost stripper of the era, was imported for the gala occasion. She performed what were vulgarly termed "belly dances" to the intense delight of as much of Seattle's male population as could pack itself inside the theater.

Considine rubbed his well-manicured hands as he observed that, in his opinion, prosperity was just around the corner. He was right, too. Once having established a foot in the door, he expanded fast and efficiently. He bought an interest in a saloon, Billy the Mug's, which is still a nostalgic tradition in a city that has never quite gotten over the urge to throw itself wide open ever so often. Billy the Mug's at Second and Washington, was the perfect symbol of a wide open town. The rooms above Billy the Mug's were operated by Considine as the Owl Club Rooms. Those not inclined to part with their bankrolls in the pursuit of wine, women or song at his other enterprises could achieve the same results bucking the games of chance at Considine's Owl Club. With his capital wisely invested in every well-paying line of Tenderloin activity, Considine turned to the important field of First Ward politics.

It was the great Gold Rush that made Tenderloin activities profitable, but it was city politics that made it possible for them to operate. Even in the closing years of the nineteenth century most of the really lucrative lines of business were more than somewhat illegal. In order to keep things booming south of Yesler Way it was essential that Seattle have a cooperative city administration; one that wouldn't keep dredging up impractical technicalities of the law and making a fuss about them. Seattle got that kind of city government after W. D. Wood, the last of the nineteenth century reform mayors, caught the gold fever and abandoned City Hall to sail north on the *Humboldt*.

When it became clear that Mayor Wood wasn't coming back for a while, the City Council pondered the choice of a suitable chief executive to take his place. They suspected that the town was tired of playing at respectability, an opinion which was soon backed up verbally and in writing by practically every organization in Seattle, from the Chamber of Commerce to the Independent Order of Good Things, which was the informal society of box house and variety theater operators. Its succinct motto was *"Skin

'Em", and John Considine was one of its moving spirits.
(Later it changed its name to the Fraternal Order of Ea-
gles and became just as respectable as the Chamber of
Commerce.)

The theory was this: hundreds of gold seekers had died
on the icy Klondike trails, partly because they had tried to
carry too much with them. Since Seattle publicity had
brought the Gold Rush there, it was Seattle's humanitarian
duty to lighten the load of the prospectors, particularly that
part which is customarily carried in wallets, money-belts or
rawhide pokes. In Honest Tom Humes the council found a
Mayor who was willing to back that public-spirited policy
one hundred percent.

Peppery Tom Humes looked exactly like Mark Twain, a
trait of which he was well aware and made the most of;
among his other political assets were a sulphurous vocabulary and an ability to out-shout almost everybody in town.
Selected as Mayor in 1897, he saw his duty and he did it.
He opened up the town.

The citizens elected him with a thumping majority the
following year and Honest Tom, who could recognize a
mandate as well as anyone, opened things up a notch or
two wider. When he was swept into office in 1900, still on
the Republican—Prosperity—Wide Open Town Ticket, he
pulled out all the stops.

The old Barbary Coast was definitely outclassed by this
time. Big gambling houses like the Totem, the Dawson,
and the Union were running day and night with three shifts
of bankers, dealers, shills and bartenders sweating to keep
up with the demand. It was the same with the girls at the
glittering parlor houses where prospective clients could
choose between one advertised as the world's largest, another which boasted of employing representatives of every
race and nationality in the civilized world, and Madam
Kate's, whose proprietress was driven to the premises by
liveried retainers, where no profanity was allowed, and free
medical attention was guaranteed any gentleman who could
prove that he had come to grief in that refined establishment.

The open door policy was staunchly backed by a majority of the City Council, led by First Ward Councilman Kist-ler and a small, active and articulate gentleman named Hiram Gill, who was the representative of the Third Ward. Of the two, Kistler probably carried the more weight, since his stamping ground, the First Ward, embraced the Ten-derloin. The respectable citizens to the north and east might forget to vote, but Kistler's constituents never did. Their livelihood was too closely linked to the tides of city government. Furthermore, the First Ward could deliver batches of well organized votes when and where they were needed. At the going rate of two dollars and a fairly good cigar, the Tenderloin was full of citizens willing to vote ex-actly as desired.

With the Mayor and the City Council as a front, the practical work of organization was carried on by private citizens of the Tenderloin, among them the affable Consi-dine, who soon gained for himself the unofficial, but influ-ential title of Boss Sport.

On the surface everything seemed smoothly organized and well under control, but below the placid depths there was turmoil. As is often the case, it was brought on by am-bition.

Honest Tom Humes, riding the crest of open town en-thusiasm, felt that he was meant for bigger things. Even when the backwoods precincts overcame the Seattle vote to deny him a United States Senate seat in 1898 he wasn't discouraged. In 1900 he decided to try for the governor-ship. This led to conflict with the city's leading Republican newspaper, the *Post-Intelligencer*, which had just changed hands again.

The new proprietor was John L. Wilson, a well-groomed ex-senator from eastern Washington who had purchased the paper with money borrowed from Jim Hill, who had brought the Great Northern to Seattle. Wilson set himself up in the business of political king-maker after making a formal announcement of his editorship in which he assured his readers that *"no corporation whatever has advanced any of the money for the purchase of this paper, directly or indirectly"*, a statement which was at least technically cor-rect. The purchase price had come from Jim Hill personally rather than from Jim Hill as represented by the Great Northern.

After an assurance that the *P. I.* still stood for the sound principles of Republicanism, the gold standard and free enterprise, Wilson closed with these words: *"We have no enemies to punish; no favorites to reward"*. That was a phrase which was to be heard frequently in the next few years.

Wilson and the *P. I.* may have had no enemies on December 7, 1899, the date of the transfer in ownership, but no time was wasted in making some. The first was Honest Tom Humes.

Since Wilson was determined to make political kings of his own, he could see no profit in backing one who was already crowned. He decided to blast Humes from the mayor's throne in the process of denying him the gubernatorial seat. The combination of adverse *P. I.* publicity and Wilson's personal influence with the state Republican organization was too much for Honest Tom. He lost the nomination to a Wilson protege named Frink. Thus began a rift in the Republican ranks which was destined to split the city of Seattle wide open.

The Humes organization fought Republican nominee Frink with a lot more violence than it fought Democrat John Rogers. The 1900 election was a Republican landslide, the state ticket riding in on the coat-tails of William McKinley and Teddy Roosevelt . . . all but Wilson's hand-picked candidate for governor. Poor Frink didn't even carry King County.

It was a mortal blow to the ambitious king-maker, and he knew just who had delivered it. The big guns of the *Post-Intelligencer* opened up full blast on Mayor Humes, hammering steadily at his vulnerable point—the vice and evil which he had permitted to twine itself about the fair city of Seattle.

For the first and probably the only time in their long and colorful history, the city's two leading dailies found themselves more or less in agreement on an issue. The *Times*, vigorously edited by Colonel Alden J. Blethen who had bought it cheap following the panic of 1893, had backed

Bryan and free silver. The Colonel was just as mad as Wilson, possibly even more so, for Colonel Blethen was a man who could get madder than almost anybody else in the State of Washington. Republican Humes was caught in the cross-fire, apparently without a friend in the journalistic world.

Faced with daily accounts of honest working men ruined by operators of wide-open gambling hells, of fallen women parading their shame on the city streets, of pickpockets and bunco artists plying their trade unmolested among the unsuspecting crowds at the Alaska steamship docks, Humes resorted to a defensive tactic frequently employed by Seattle mayors. He adroitly passed the buck to Chief of Police C. S. Reed.

When queried by the *P. I.*, Reed said emphatically that he wasn't planning to resign. *"I do my duty as I see it"*, the chief said stoutly, *"and without fear or favor. I have no enemies to punish and no favorites to reward"*. After that lofty if not original sentiment he added practically, *"Anyway I have no business in which to engage except the police business"*.

Shortly thereafter Mayor Humes graciously accepted the resignation which Chief Reed still hadn't offered him.

Seattle's new Chief of Police was a short, dapper young man with a highly respectable background. William L. Meredith was the son of Captain William M. Meredith, a prominent member of the Grand Army of the Republic, a personal friend of President Harrison, in whose civil war regiment he had commanded a company, and director of the U. S. Bureaus of Printing and Engraving. The younger Meredith had come to Seattle to look after the affairs of an eastern capitalist who had taken over most of the Seattle property reclaimed by the government from Doc Maynard. He stayed on as a "Chinese Inspector" in the U. S. Customs Service, transferring from there to a job as detective on the Seattle police force. During John Considine's first venture in the Tenderloin box house field, Meredith quit the force to work for him, following him to eastern Washington and coming back with him to Seattle for his highly successful second try.

Meredith discovered that the box house business wasn't the only line of activity that had become profitable since the start of the Gold Rush. The detective business was good, too. He quit Considine to return to the force, where he became closely associated with a newcomer to the ranks of Seattle's plain clothesmen, a short, rotund, tough individual named C. W. Wappenstein, former chief of police of Cincinnati, Ohio.

It was more or less an unwritten law in the department that the established businesses of the Tenderloin were to add a bit of butter and jam to the daily bread of the uniformed division, while the detectives were to confine their financial activities to the pickpockets and confidence men, of whom there were an abundance. A few of the best had gone north to Skagway with Soapy Smith, where they sold gold-plated bricks and other people's mining claims, and even took over the local Army recruiting office in order to remove valuables from the clothing of patriotic young men who were taking physical examinations, but there were plenty left in Seattle.

Meredith sewed the seeds of his own destruction when he arrested one of the city's leading pickpockets who was also a personal friend of Considine. The dip complained bitterly to the Boss Sport that he had been framed, having paid Meredith his regular license fee shortly before his arrest. Considine couldn't stand a dishonest cop and this was a double-cross of the worst sort. In a few days Meredith was processing stray dog reports behind a row of filing cabinets at headquarters. He still drew a full detective's pay—ninety dollars a month—but he was in disgrace and, what was worse, he was forced to live within the limits of the monthly insult which the city gave him in lieu of a proper pay check. He wrote the name or John Considine at the top of the list in his little black book.

The Boss Sport knew just where he stood with Meredith, so it was quite a blow to him when the dapper detective was named to succeed Reed as Chief of Police. Considine braced himself for trouble, which wasn't long in coming.

It had been police policy to enforce the vice laws rigorously in certain areas, thus building up the arrest figures and throwing up a virtuous smoke screen to impress the advocates of law and order. Chinatown had been the favorite location for previous raids, largely because the Chinese gambling house proprietors refused to pay for protection. They felt it was cheaper and more fun to build secret passages, false doors and hidden stairways to confuse the police, and they did it so well that they even became confused themselves at times. Detectives Wappenstein and Powers were specialists in threading the Oriental mazes of Chinatown, but when Meredith became chief he sicked them on the Boss Sport along with most of the rest of the force. Practically all the law enforcement in Seattle was suddenly concentrated on the Considine enterprises.

This enraged the Boss Sport and failed to placate the *Post-Intelligencer*. The City Council decided to see if there was really any improper activity going on south of Yesler Way. They conducted a top secret investigation which was reported in the greatest detail by the newspapers, especially the *P. I.* The hearings developed into a mud-slinging duel between Considine and Meredith. Wilson took the Boss Sport to his bosom and the *Post-Intelligencer's* columns pictured him as a sort of civic Robin Hood. The *Times* backed Meredith because Colonel Blethen instinctively disagreed with the *P. I.* whenever it was humanly possible to do so and because Colonel Blethen didn't like John Considine.

Considine provided the Council with eye-witness reports of graft payments made to Meredith henchmen and delivered to the chief. The *P. I.* gave this testimony full play.

Then Meredith and the *Times* had their turn. The Chief of Police charged that Considine had "ruined" a teen-age girl performer at the People's Theater, with the result that she required an operation which was financed by Considine. When Considine countered with proof that the young artist, who was a contortionist, had merely ruptured herself in the course of her professional duties, more evidence was produced to show that Considine was a bad influence on Seattle girlhood. Another teen-ager, one Beera Beebe, billed at the People's as Zephyrine, had been rescued from ex-Mayor Wood's steamer *Humboldt* in the nick of time, having been decoyed aboard by Swiftwater Bill Gates.

Considine admitted that Zephyrine's parents had rescued her from the clutches of Swiftwater Bill just as the *Humboldt*'s gangplank was being drawn in, but he denied any responsibility. Swiftwater Bill, who was the most publicized of the fabulous Gold Rush millionaires, had aroused Zephyrine's girlish emotions by tossing twenty dollar gold pieces to the chorus line at the People's, later going back stage when Zephyrine wasn't looking and forcing all the other girls to give theirs back.

At the close of the hearing the Council informed Mayor Humes that his Chief of Police was unfit for office, it having been established that "Money has been paid to Meredith and Detective Wappenstein for the privilege of conducting bunco and 'sure thing' games in the city undisturbed".

Honest Tom, the poor man's Mark Twain, looked as pained as if he were the original and had just been informed that Tom Sawyer was a juvenile delinquent. Shaking his gray mane sadly, he sent word to Meredith that Seattle was going to have a new Chief of Police; at headquarters Meredith dispatched Detective Powers, recently promoted to police sergeant, to purchase a sawed off shotgun. Then he sat down to write his resignation.

If there had been any doubt in Meredith's mind as to what he was going to do with the shotgun, it was removed when, forty-eight hours later, he was informed that unless he had a public apology printed on the front page of the *Times* Considine was going to sue him for libel. When the ultimatum was delivered Meredith's face flushed and then turned deadly pale. *"I've lost my job"*, he muttered, *"and now this"*.

The next day, Tuesday, June 25, Considine left his office at the People's in mid-afternoon. He thought he was catching a cold; he felt a little feverish and his throat was raw. Before he left he took a .38 revolver from his desk and thrust it into the buckskin gun pocket sewed inside the waistband of his trousers. Word was out on the grapevine that Meredith was in a killing mood.

Considine started walking north on Second Avenue toward Yesler where he could catch a cable car for home. At the car stop he met his brother, Tom. They stood idly on the corner for a few minutes watching Ralph Hopkins making a flying start for the First Street Hill in his Woods Electric—the only horseless carriage in town. The electric was almost out of sight by the time it bogged down on the grade, but the Considine brothers agreed that automobiles would never amount to very much in Seattle.[1]

Up around Pike Street Meredith was walking south on Second Avenue and he was a one-man arsenal. He carried a big Colt revolver at his hip, a bulldog .38 in one pocket, a wicked stiletto in another, and the paper-wrapped shotgun was cradled in his arms.

It was a stage-setting for tragedy, but it was ludicrous, too. The ex-Police Chief stalked Second Avenue like the caricature of a Western marshal going out to rid the town of its Bad Man, but festooned as he was with weapons, the dapper little man looked comical instead of grim. He was out of character in another way too. Instead of stalking his enemy silently, he paused at every opportunity to discuss his plans. "I'm looking for Considine. This town's not big enough to hold us both", he told people who questioned him. "He got me out of my job and now I'm going to kill the son-of-a-bitch".

The Boss Sport wasn't at the cable car stop when Meredith got there. He and his brother had just left for Guy's Drug Store at Second and Yesler to pick up a bottle of cough medicine. Meredith saw them crossing the street and went after them. The Considines met a uniformed policeman at the drug store door, an Officer Merford who had been suspended by Meredith for pocketing part of a protection payment earmarked for the Chief.

This patrolman, having no great love for the ex-Chief, was pumping Considine's arm and telling him what an unprincipled little so-and-so Meredith was, when he was somewhat startled to see Meredith himself standing beside him

---

[1] That first Seattle automobile ended up in Tacoma, where it can still be seen at the State Historical Society Museum.

with a sawed off shotgun leveled at the man whose hand he was shaking. The shotgun blasted a charge of heavy buckshot at Considine's head from a distance of two feet.

The deafening blast and shock convinced Patrolman Merford and Considine's brother Tom that they had been shot too, but as a matter of fact no one had been hit. The buckshot charge didn't have space to spread. It passed over the Boss Sport's shoulder to knock a large chunk of ceiling onto the heads of startled customers inside the store.

Big John Considine, six feet tall and imposing as any banker in his sober broadcloth and neat brown derby, stumbled through the swinging wooden doors, followed by little William Meredith, who shoved past Tom Considine and Merford, both too stunned to do much of anything except reel around and wonder when they would start to bleed.

Meredith took aim again, firing at Considine's broad back. As he pulled the trigger the swinging door flew back, jogging his elbow. One pellet hit Considine in the neck, but the rest of the charge smashed through the arm of a messenger boy at the soda fountain before it went on to shatter medicine bottles all over amazed Dr. G. O. Guy in the prescription department.

Dropping the empty shotgun, Meredith reached for the heavy revolver at his hip. Considine was trapped between the showcases, bellowing for help, but when he saw that help wouldn't be coming in time to do him any good he swung into action. Leaping upon Meredith before he could fire, Considine used his weight advantage to push the smaller man back toward the front of the store while keeping his gun arm pinioned.

Tom Considine, convinced at last that he was still alive, pushed his way in to twist the gun from Meredith's hand, using it to club the little man savagely on the head. The King County sheriff and a city detective arrived then to jerk the gun away, but not before Meredith was sagging against a counter with his skull fractured.

Tom regained the gun with a sudden lunge, using it to force back the growing crowd that was entering the store. John drew his own .38 then and shot Meredith three times from so close a range that the burning powder set his victim's coat on fire. Meredith was dead. The sheriff took Considine's gun and said "You're under arrest, John". The Boss Sport nodded. The whole drama, from start to finish, had lasted just a minute and a half by the clock on the drug store wall.

Considine was declared not guilty of the charge against him—first degree murder—in the trial that followed. The *P. I.* praised the jury warmly, while the *Times* observed darkly that open season appeared to have been declared on police officers.

Considine, although a free man, discovered that the Tenderloin was no longer the lucrative field for him that it once had been. For reasons of self-preservation if no others, policemen are prone to look with disfavor on known cop-killers. The Boss Sport found his enterprises suffering from an over-abundance of police attention, and gradually he drifted into more legitimate operations. He rode to new success on the nickelodeon craze, parlaying the primitive five cent flicker palaces into a string of first-class vaudeville and movie houses that covered the West. In a later all-out fight for supremacy, Considine lost out to an enterprising Greek named Pericles Pantages, who in turn sold the circuit to RKO for twenty-five million dollars. The Boss Sport ended his days in California as a highly respected and reasonably wealthy motion picture producer.[2]

In spite of the fulminations of the *Post-Intelligencer* and the only slightly less pointed barbs of the *Times*, Honest Tom Humes lasted for three full terms in addition to the partial one he had served as a City Council appointee. His reign didn't end until 1904, and there was never a dull moment.

Things became especially noisy in the spring of 1902

---

[2] John Considine became a respected business man, but he never quite lost his sporting blood. When he built the $300,000 Orpheum Theater in later years he awarded the $15,000 architectural contract by the flip of a silver dollar. Architect William Kingsley won the toss—and the job—from E. W. Houghton. According to the *Times* it was "nearly, if not quite, the largest bunch of money that ever changed hands in Seattle on a game of chance".

when a previously-unknown gambling house operator began to make headlines with a charge that he had been double-crossed by the Mayor. The gambler's name was Tex Rickard, but it wasn't a familiar name to the reporters, who sometimes spelled it Rickards. This new arrival to the Tenderloin claimed that he had been promised a free hand in the gambling line in return for a thousand dollar contribution which he made to the campaign fund of Honest Tom. On the strength of that assurance, he had expended an additional sizable sum in properly fitting out his place of business at First Avenue South and Washington Street. When he was ready to open the doors, however, he was informed by Chief of Police Sullivan, latest of the Humes appointees, that it was against the law to gamble in Seattle.

Understandably indignant, Rickard demanded that he either get his money back or be furnished with a ticket to do business in his chosen profession. When no inclination was shown to provide him with either, he yelled for a lawyer. The lawyer was the ubiquitous Councilman from the Third Ward, Hiram Gill.

Gill was a seasoned campaigner, having long been a defender of the Tenderloin's downtrodden. He called the newspapers to tell them of the dirty trick that had been played on his latest client and to explain what he proposed to do about it. He was duly quoted in the next editions:

"Hiram C. Gill, member of the city council from the Third Ward, and as well the attorney for Tex Rickard, the gambler, may make a great stir in the council at its next meeting tomorrow night over the gambling situation. At least, according to his own statement, he is thinking seriously of raising trouble. He hopes to have Chief of Police Sullivan removed unless certain things are done that his client Tex Rickard wants done. Mr. Gill's plan is to ask for a council investigation of the conduct of the chief of police toward gamblers; to demand from the chief an explanation of why he allows some men to gamble and refuses permits to others. Unless the chief is able to explain that point Mr. Gill has intimated that he will immediately demand the chief's removal under section 28 of Ordinance 5657, approved November 17, 1899".

The ordinance was then solemnly reproduced for the edification of a citizenry which could hardly have been unaware that its city was the undisputed gambling capital of America:

"The chief of police and every police officer of the City of Seattle must inform against and diligently watch for, search out and promptly arrest or cause to be arrested, all persons whom they have good cause to believe are offending against the provisions of this ordinance (relating to gambling), and every such officer refusing to do so shall be deemed guilty of a misdemeanor and shall be punished by a fine of not more than $100 and be summarily removed from office by the city council of the said city".

It was Gill's contention that if the ordinance was going to be enforced to stop Rickard it was going to be enforced to stop everybody, or he was going to know the reason why.

Mayor Humes responded that it was his policy to leave law enforcement in the hands of the Chief of Police, a statement which caused Sullivan to glance nervously about on the suspicion that the buck might be due for another fast pass. When pressed further, Humes let it be known that the Dexter Horton Bank had complained about a gambling house being opened up practically next door, that he knew nothing about Tex Rickard's thousand dollars, and that, on general principles, he had no enemies to punish and no friends to reward.

This failed to appease Hiram Gill, Tex Rickard or the newspapers. Gill threatened to close up every gambling house in town, oust the Chief of Police and bring impeachment proceedings against the Mayor. *"I'm going to make that bird lay down his hand"*, said Gill, referring to the city's chief executive, *"and I'm going to follow the spoor of John Sullivan until I find out it he's a real chief of police or a stool pigeon for a dissolute mayor and errand boy for a gang of gamblers".*

A *Times* reporter, scratching away hard to keep up with the eloquent Gill, interposed with a leading question. *"I suppose that you are prompted to this move through the al-*

leged injustice done your client Tex Rickard?" the news-man asked.

"Then," the *Times* chronicled dramatically, *"Gill wheeled in his chair, and bringing his long bony finger down in a most emphatic gesture, said: 'I am not in any way connected with Tex Rickard. No matter whether in the past I have been his attorney or not, I can now say honest-ly that in the present instance I have severed all connection with that man. Any moves I make from now on will be strictly on my own hook. Using Mayor Humes' pet phrase, I may say I have neither friends to reward nor enemies to punish' "*.

Well embarked on the wings of oratory, the councilman then made a somewhat surprising statement: *"Unless gam-bling is run on a fair and square basis I am going to see that Seattle is minus her gambling hells, which, at best, are the blackest blots she has ever had upon her name"*.

The reporter then asked a logical question which stopped Gill momentarily. *"Aside from the injustice of this one instance, how do you personally stand on the gambling question?"*

The councilman swallowed several times, perhaps men-tally eating the noble words he had just uttered. *"The city needs the revenue"*, he said at last, *"personally and for the financial good of the city, I'm in favor of gambling"*.

And that probably still stands as the fastest flipflop ever made in the history of Seattle politics.

The head of the local Republican Campaign Committee didn't deny that he had accepted Rickard's controversial thousand dollars, but he indicated that he would swallow it before he'd give it back. He was underrating Hiram Charles Gill, city councilman and attorney at law.

Hi was undersized and scrawny, with a big head, weak eyes and an uninspiring countenence. Tex Rickard's friend, Wilson Mizner, is said to have described Gill as nothing but a trellis for vericose veins, and even his ardent admir-ers admitted that Hi was a mite on the puny side.

But Hi was a fighter and Seattle has always admired a fighter. It's a city that has always had a soft spot in its heart for a character, too, as it has proven in more recent political campaigns. Hi made himself into a character. Pipe smoke made him sick to his stomach, but he learned to smoke a corncob. Newspaper cartoonists loved it and that corncob pipe became a symbol of Hi Gill. He affected unpressed pants, farmer-style galoshes and a white string tie topped by an oversized Western hat.

Hi Gill reacted to publicity with all the shy reserve of a cat wallowing in a catnip bed and the Rickard case was a publicity bonanza which he mined diligently for all it was worth. The established gamblers who, according to many well-informed sources, were using the Mayor and the police to force a newly-arrived competitor out of business, became perturbed at the unrelenting blasts from Hi Gill. They wanted an atmosphere of peace and quiet above all else. Finally, taking another look at the flashy stranger, they came to the conclusion that, in the interests of fair play and business ethics, he should get his money back.

Eventually he did, although from what source history does not record. Having obtained it, Rickard embarked upon the *Oregon* northbound for Dawson City. He did not return to Seattle's Tenderloin, although stories of his exploits in the North did trickle down from time to time. One of the classics involved his friend Mizner. Tex had taken a fancy to a fancy lady named Goldie who was notorious throughout the northern-lights districts. One night Mizner approached a hotel just as a frightened man came leaping through the front door with Rickard in hot pursuit. Tex blazed away wildly with a big revolver, but the stranger escaped in the dark. The town was thrown into great confusion. "What happened?" men asked excitedly as they dashed toward the hotel. Tex looked noble and heroic. "He insulted Goldie!" he explained in outraged tones. The crowd buzzed and chattered with excitement. Again Tex bellowed, *"He insulted Goldie!"*

Through the crowd came Mizner. "For God's sake, *how?*" he inquired in honest wonderment.

Even the departure from Seattle of such colorful personalities as these left the newspapers with no dearth of interesting material. Later in the summer the escaped convict,

Harry Tracy came to Seattle, through the dark pall of burning forests, to engage in a running gun fight with posses from Bothell to Renton. Tracy escaped across the Cascades, leaving a trail of dead and wounded law officers behind him, but King County Sheriff Cudihee was following him like an avenging spirit, giving the legendary outlaw no rest until, on the evening of August 8, Tracy was shot down in a Lincoln County wheat field.

After the Tracy hysteria was over Colonel Blethen sent a reporter on a round of pavilions and refreshment stands at the city parks along Lake Washington. The dedicated journalist was served with beer and hard liquor at Leschi, wandered down to Madison where he had a few for the road, and then returned under his own power, although weaving slightly, to announce that liquor was flowing as freely in the public parks as in the Tenderloin. He added somewhat plaintively, however, that the quality of the stuff they served you in the parks wasn't nearly as high.

Having learned of this problem, which was presented by the *Times* in no uncertain terms, the City Council proposed to solve it in a forthright manner; they would license the park bootleggers—blind pig operators they called them in those days—thus legalizing them and bringing added license fees to the city in one masterful stroke.

Colonel Blethen believed in a wide open restricted district, on the theory that you can't legislate sin out of existence, but he wanted it concentrated in one place. The rest of the town was to be kept respectable at any cost. Furthermore, the Colonel had been plumping for a city ordinance raising saloon license fees to a thousand dollars a year. Since the town had hundreds of them, that would bring in a pretty penny, relieving honest businessmen of a major share of the tax burden. This was just what he had been waiting for. He pointed out that the Council was willing to license hell fire and damnation in the city parks for a few paltry dollars a year, but refused to pass his thousand dollar saloon license. He inferred that the tainted gold of saloon men and brewers was a major influence upon the city fathers.

Councilman Kistler of the First Ward, whom the *Times*

referred to as *"the self-appointed revenue watch-dog of the city treasury and imperial somersault artist of the city council"* evaded the high license issue with a revenue-raising suggestion which left the Colonel almost, but not quite, wordless with indignation. Mr. Kistler suggested a city tax on ping pong tables!

The Colonel didn't get the saloon license fee boosted, but his lurid stories of the "blind pigs" in the parks brought the law and order league out in force, frightening the City Council into reversing its decision to grant them permits.

Amid the uproar Honest Tom Humes hewed diligently to the line he had set for himself. When the Chamber of Commerce sent a committee to expostulate with him on the grounds that maybe he had opened things up just a teeny bit *too* wide, the Mayor lit into them unmercifully. The committee members were unable to get a word in, edgeways or otherwise, and they left with ruffled feathers to report to their parent body that the Mayor had left them with the definite feeling that they had been "sat down upon".

Honest Tom had been elected to run an open town, and that's the way he ran it, but he was proud of one thing. He forced the streetcar company to build a number of sprinkling cars, which rolled along the city's thoroughfares flushing the refuse into the gutters.

Standing outside City Hall to watch one of the first water cars clank by with all streams spouting, the Mayor turned proudly to the group of citizens around him.

"Look at that", said Honest Tom. "Before I'm through we'll have the cleanest city in the United States!"

UP BY THE BOOTSTRAPS

IT'S EASY TO LOSE perspective when you peer back through the mists of time and try to figure out how things got the way they are. The gaudy and sensational make better copy than the solid plodding that builds a city, but all Seattle's headlines weren't being made in the Tenderloin. Seattle had rebuilt itself from almost total destruction, doubling its population in the process. After that the city began to pull itself up by its own bootstraps . . . out of the mud and out of the natural cage of hills that had kept it penned on the tideflats for the first half century of its development.

The district south of Yesler Way, the bawdy, brawling, gaudy Tenderloin, was just a disreputable offshoot of something that was going on from one end to the other of the sprawling young city on the hills above Elliott Bay. Seattle was growing faster than any city had ever grown before, spreading like a forest fire, swelling like a neap tide flooding a narrow beach, reproducing cells like an ameoba . . . doubling and redoubling itself and then redoubling itself again before there was time to so much as take a census. Seattle was growing too fast to take time out for niceties. Seattle bragged and boasted and showed its muscles to the world, in the manner of a strong and growing child. Likewise, Seattle was something of a bully, snatching prizes from the other Northwest towns that had failed to keep pace in the race for supremacy.

In 1890 the city directory, the first published since the Great Fire and the second in the city's history, listed the population at 43,000 as compared to 19,000 the year before the fire. In 1900 the population was over 80,000. In 1910 it was over two hundred thousand.

The bouncing infant city of 1890, like any baby, was living in the present, unaware that it had any past and willing to let the future take care of itself. There hadn't been time to reflect on history, and there was nothing legendary about the pilgrim fathers who had come ashore in the November rain to build a city from one log cabin without a roof. The cabin was still standing at Alki Point, if anybody cared to look at it,[1] and you could call the pilgrim fathers on the telephone; the more progressive of them anyway. Arthur Denny was the first to bow to progress, with telephone number 9 listed for his fine new mansion at 1328 Front Street, but stubborn old Henry Yesler would have no part of the new-fangled device. Judge Burke, of course, had a telephone in his room at the Rainier Club—you could reach him at 30—but Dexter Horton compromised by having one only at his office.

Most of the city's fathers had adapted themselves to push-button lighting, too, and if there was drama in the contrast between that first smoky driftwood fire in the roofless cabin at Alki Point and the electric chandeliers of their new mansions, they were too busy to reflect upon it. The founding fathers had picked a winner and they were cashing in on it.

From 1890 to 1900 Seattle grew wildly and without much plan, almost choking itself in its attempt to expand within the narrow boundaries that denied expansion . . . the towering hills to the east, the deep harbor to the west. There was neither time nor space for

---

[1] It was about this time that Arthur Denny tried to interest the town in buying and preserving the historic Alki Point log cabin, but there was little response. The cabin was burned by the owner of the property in 1893.

sthetic matters. Energy was being expended to build new
rick and stone buildings, five, six and even seven stories
igh, but their foundations were in the mud. The fir plank-
ng of the streets was ground away and seldom replaced.
he winter rains ran like dirty cascades down the hill
treets into the business district. The *Post-Intelligencer*
ublished a stirring editorial urging Seattle women to defy
he fashion edicts of the East and raise the hemlines of
heir dresses at least an inch or two above ground level.
he editor said it depressed him to watch the female popu-
ation floundering about in skirts that dragged in the mud
o grow heavier and more bedraggled at every step.

He kept the discussion on a high plane, asserting that
here is nothing inherently immoral in the display of the
emale foot, even when muddy, and assuring his gentle
eaders that if they followed his advice they would find
hemselves admired for their common sense as much as for
heir well turned ankles.

There was no editorial comment when a ten-year-old
oy named Joseph Bufonchio drowned in the malodorous
ink-hole which was the southeast corner of Jackson and
hird Avenue at the turn of the century. The reporter who
overed the incident seemed to consider accidental drown-
ngs in Seattle's city streets as more or less routine trage-
ies, although he did comment on the unusually large
rowd which gathered to watch policemen and a few volun-
eers probe the mud for the boy's body. He estimated the
rowd at 2000, give or take a dozen or so, and everyone
vas vastly entertained when the boy's father arrived on the
cene and, in his grief and anxiety, fell into the mudhole
hat had killed his son.

"Several other laughable incidents happened", the re-
orter added whimsically. A local pugilist named "Chicago
3d" hooked a snag which he thought was the body, and in
is struggles to lift it from the murky depths, he too fell in
he water to the further delight of the crowd.

The cable cars did their best to help the city expand upward, but they were like the rest of Seattle—straining the
ast pound of energy to keep up with runaway population
igures and cope with the restricting hills that hampered ra-

tional growth. Sometimes they, like the city streets, gav
way under the pressure. A James Street dummy, inboun
from Athletic Park with a rain-soaked crowd of footba
fans covering every square inch of its interior, sides an
roof, helped usher out the closing months of the 90's b
dropping its cable and hurtling over the precipice at to
speed. With its gong hammering hysterically and sheddin
passengers like confetti, the little car seemed determined t
make the salt water dive so long predicted by the prophet
of doom. The gripman managed to reengage the runnin
gear and wind the brake down tight before final disaste
overtook him, but by that time he was the only one lef
aboard the once crowded car. And when the stop wa
made it was of such a sudden nature that he went hurtlin
over the front platform to plow a furrow in the mudd
street.

It was sensational, but when all the scattered passenger
were accounted for it was found that nobody had bee
killed, which was typical of Seattle. Probably no other cit
has such a genius for staging violent and even appallin
spectacles without many casualties. The Indian War result
ed in only two deaths, the Chinese riots in only one, an
even the Great Fire, as far as could be determined, claime
no lives.[2]

Things followed the same pattern when Judge Burke'
long-suffering electric generator celebrated the coming o
the 20th century by flying apart spectacularly in the earl
months of 1900. Sam Shuffleton had made it perform mira
cles down in the basement of the Burke Building at Secon
and Marion, pulling elevators up and down, making ligh
bulbs glow and powering the Ballard streetcars, but like Se
attle, it was reaching the bursting point. It finally let g
with a bang that shook the solid brick building. Blue spark
buzzed across the basement while the premises lit up an
vibrated like a berserk pinball machine. Flywheels ra

---

[2] A few fragments of a human body were sieved out of the ash
es of what had been Chinatown, but investigation proved these t
be the remains of an embalmed Oriental who had been awaitin
shipment to the home soil.

wild, snapping belts which whipped about dangerously.

The new paid fire department arrived on the scene without delay, but the firemen decided this was out of their line. Eventually Sam Shuffleton put in an appearance, traveling at the long lope of a fond father who has just been notified that his only child has been kicked by a horse. Into the smoking, flashing, flailing shambles he plunged without a moment's hesitation. Everyone on Second Avenue breathed a long sigh of relief when Shuffleton made it to the master switch and shut off the fireworks. People who witnessed that drama in Judge Burke's basement were not surprised when, in later years, Sam Shuffleton emerged as a top figure in the electrical business and had a huge powerhouse named after him.

Almost everything in the Seattle of 1900 was like the Burke Building generator—carrying a greater load than it was designed for. Down on the waterfront the Alaska steamers lined the shaky, wooden docks, unloading a steady stream of gold while they embarked new hordes of north-bound treasure seekers. The waterfront streets were rutted quagmires traversed by jostling fleets of drays, express wagons, delivery vans and hacks. Traffic congestion along the waterfront on steamer days reached peaks never equalled in the automobile age, and no one had thought of one-way streets.

Sometimes the confusion on the waterfront spread to unexpected places, as when a small boy driving a large horse and loaded express wagon tried to take a shortcut through the alley behind Sherman, Clay and Company's store on Second Avenue. Finding he had entered a deadend driveway, the boy began the delicate maneuver of turning the wagon around in the narrow passage. In the process he backed the clumsy vehicle into the open doorway of a large chute used for sliding pianos from the alley to the music store's downstairs showrooms. Prospective piano buyers, listening to an aria being played by an elderly lady at a new Steinway, were horrified to observe a large perplexed horse slide smoothly into their midst, preceded by a fully loaded express wagon and a boy in the last stages of profane frustration. It was necessary, eventually, to lead the horse and wagon through the store and out the main entrance on Second Avenue. This created a further sensation, especially among the patrons of neighboring saloons, a number of whom made immediate pledges of total abstinence.

The *Post-Intelligencer* summed up the annoyances attendant upon the city's weedlike growth: *"As the population and business of Seattle increase, the question of traffic on the streets and passage along the sidewalks becomes more and more important.*

"There are certain classes of people who will sooner or later have to curb their propensities or suffer the consequences. At present they are simply an inconvenient nuisance. There is the man who persists in turning to the left when he meets people on the street or sidewalk. He will swing down the sidewalk for two or three blocks, keeping carefully to the left, and of course coming into contact with nine tenths of the people he meets.

"There is the reckless bicycle rider. Boys go scorching down Cherry Street, on the slope from Second to First Avenue, at an alarming rate, and it is only a question of time when there will be a serious collision at the corner.[3]

"There is the careless driver who rushes his team through Pioneer Place with as much abandon as if he were driving along a country road.

"There are the men who crowd the platforms of street cars, though there is plenty of room inside. There are women who make life on the street miserable with long-handled umbrellas and cumbrous baby carriages. There are men who barricade the doors of office buildings and hotels. There are restaurant waiters whose supreme object seems to be to cultivate in their patrons the virtue of patience.

"To all these, and to some others, two little words that were much in use in Chicago when the large crowds were attending the World's Fair would appeal with special force,

---

[3] That Cherry Street hill had always been a problem. It took an extra horse to help the first street cars up the one-block incline and teams were always running away on the down-grade. In 1892 a two-horse wagon, loaded with dirt from the new opera house site at Third and Cherry, ended up in the lobby of the Merchant's National Bank at the foot of the street.

as the pulse of Seattle's commercial and civic life beats more and more quickly each day. The words, as heard on Chicago street cars, in the buildings and on the street corners were 'STEP LIVELY!' ".

Seattle was stepping lively at the turn of the century; the problem was one of direction rather than speed. The city needed guidance to move its unbounded energy and enthusiasm in the right direction and it got it from a prim looking civil engineer named Reginald H. Thomson. Thomson, who had come West in 1881 to survey the roadbed for Judge Burke's Lakeshore and Eastern Railroad, was a sort of Paul Bunyan in celluloid collar and spectacles. He specialized in changing the face of the earth and his plastic surgery shaped the Seattle that we know today.

Thomson was appointed city engineer a couple of years after the Great Fire. His first job was digging a sewer, a duty which he performed in a way which was to set a pattern for most of his future projects. He dug the sewer in a town of forty thousand, but he dug it for a city ten times that large. The professional croakers and militant taxpayers set up a pitiful wailing and gnashing of teeth over the mad extravagance of "that man Thomson", who was investing real dollars in the future that was still just a dream.

Thomson was just getting started. He built a pipeline from Cedar River, in the foothills of the Cascade Mountains, to Seattle, giving the city an unlimited supply of sparkling pure water. It tasted better than the stuff that had been pumped out of Lake Washington, but the small, well-organized groups which, then as now, acted as self-appointed watchdogs of the city treasury, began to beat their breasts and tear their hair in real earnest. When Thomson talked the City Council into acquiring 80,000 acres of land to form a pollution-free watershed, the baying of the watchdogs became semi-hysterical.

Thomson, however, was not listening. He was busy working on plans for washing mountains into the sea.

Seattle's hills had long been the delight of poetical citizens, who counted seven of them and were fond of drawing analogies between their young city and Rome. But they were frustrating to practical people who were trying to build a big city where there was only space for a small town. Until Thomson came along, the hills were classed with the weather—something you talk about but can't do anything about. Thomson decided that something *had* to be done about them. Otherwise Seattle would never grow big enough to fit the water and sewage systems he had built for it.

Denny Hill was the worst. Sloping upward from the vicinity of Lake Union, it terminated in a high, steep bluff near Pike Street. The bluff was crowded by the ornate wooden Hotel Washington, which was the city's pride and joy.

This legendary hostelry, first known as the Denny Hotel, was modernized and renamed the Washington in later years, reopening its imposing doors in May of 1903, just in time to welcome President Teddy Roosevelt as one of its first guests. It was Teddy's first visit to the Great Northwest and he was amazed at both the elegance of his hotel and the caliber of the hecklers who attended his speeches. The lusty President, sometimes referred to in later days as Roosevelt the First, was usually able to more than hold his own in the free-for-all politics of his day, but an unknown Skid Roader was his downfall in Seattle. The shabby heckler kept interrupting the President's speech with shouts of "I'm a Socialist!".

Teddy tried to ignore him for a while, but finally he felt that he had to do something. "May I ask the gentleman *why* he is a Socialist?" he asked politely.

"My paw was a Socialist, my grampaw was a Socialist and I'm a Socialist!" the unabashed heckler replied.

"And suppose", the President thundered with glittering teeth and spectacles, "your paw had been a jackass and your grampaw had been a jackass! What would you be?"

Without hesitation the heckler yelled back, *"A Republican!"*

The Denny Hotel had more than Roosevelt legends to endear it to the heart of Seattle. The view from its spacious and secluded grounds above the city was superb. From its huge Red Parlor to its harem-like Turkish Smoking Room, it was the acme of Victorian luxury. The private tramway which carried guests from street level to hotel grounds was cherished as "the shortest streetcar line in the world". Thomson evoked more cries of anguish when he proposed to remove both hotel and bluff, but it had to be admitted that Denny Hill was a hopeless roadblock to the city's expansion northward to Lake Union. In the same manner Dearborn Hill stopped progress toward Lake Washington, while Jackson Hill towered between the city and its rich agricultural hinterland along the valley of the White River. Street grades up these barriers ran as high as twenty percent.

Thomson had logic on his side and, as is usually the case, logic eventually overcame sentiment. It was a tougher problem to get funds from the City Council to start the job of hill removing. Even if they provided the money, the councilmen wanted to know, how did Thomson think he was going to perform a vanishing act with young mountains, which weren't to be confused with children's sandpiles?

Thomson knew just how he was going to do it. He had found the solution to his problem in the hydraulic mining, used by miners to sluice gold from Alaskan soil. The same sort of huge hoses shooting jets of high-pressure water could be used to wash bothersome hills into Elliott Bay. Denny Hill was attacked first. Five million yards of dirt were sluiced down to fill the tideflats and provide level ground for industrial expansion. Another five million cubic yards came off Dearborn and Jackson Hills. Seattle surged north and south like a suddenly released tidal wave, engulfing suburban towns like Fremont, Ballard, West Seattle, Georgetown and Ravenna Park, which had been separate municipalities.[4]

Thomson had an idea that a growing city needed something besides passable streets and adequate sewers too. He

---

[4] Legendary "Belltown" was never a separate city. It was the name given to William Bell's land claim between Arthur Denny's claim on the south and David Denny's on the north and was a part of the original town of Seattle. Bell Street was one of the boundaries of this claim.

sold the City Council on the idea of hiring a nationally known firm of landscape architects, the Olmsted Brothers, to make a park and recreational survey of the city. The Olmsted report was adopted in 1903, and it was a historic event. It meant that Seattle was destined to be a beautiful city instead of just a big city.

The Olmsted plan came in time to save the southern shoreline of Lake Washington for public use. It gave Seattle the Lake Washington Boulevard, and Seward Park. It established Green Lake as a priceless beauty spot in the heart of the city. The howls of the pessimists continued, sometimes reaching a crescendo, as in 1900 when Woodland Park was purchased from the Phinney estate for a hundred thousand dollars. Court action was brought against the City Council to prevent the frittering away of public funds on a remote tract of land too far away from town to ever be of any real use to the citizens of Seattle.

But Seattle was off on another wave of optimism and the sad howling of the watchdogs was hardly heard amid the general enthusiasm. The people liked the Olmsted plan and they were willing to back it up with hard cash. Millions of dollars worth of park bonds were approved by the voters in the same years that the hills were being sluiced into the sea.

The muddy downtown streets gave way to macadam and concrete. Even the Tenderloin got a new surface. It was suggested that the name be changed to "The New Paved District" and that the honkytonks and brothels should be moved out to make way for a legitimate community of wholesale and jobbing houses. It was announced in 1902 that definite plans had been formed to move the Tenderloin to a district then known as Blackchapel, an area bounded by Fifth and Sixth, Jackson and Lane. The announcement caused property values there to skyrocket, but it was a short-lived boom. When the owners of property south of Yesler Way discovered that prostitution paid far better rents than produce they put a quiet but effective stop to all plans for the rehabilitation of the original Tenderloin.

City Engineer Thomson made a new city out of Seattle

and, in the process, he made a number of enemies, among them Colonel Alden J. Blethen of the *Times*. The Colonel arrived in Seattle between the Panic of 1893 and the Gold Rush of 1897, a period when the crashing of bankrupt businesses was echoing from all of Seattle's seven hills. He bought the *Times* just as it was about to become engulfed in a tide of red ink. He made the paper pay dividends and in the process he made his voice heard above the roar of booming Seattle.

The Colonel was a short, stout gentleman with a large head and a vast mane of frizzy hair. He also had a choleric disposition and an earthy vocabulary. It was the age of two-fisted personal journalism and Colonel Blethen could get just as two-fisted and personal as it's possible for a journalist to be. His principal antagonist was the *Post-Intelligencer*, particularly after 1904 when Erastus Brainerd, Seattle's superpress agent, took over as editor of the morning paper. Blethen and Brainerd detested each other cordially and neither of them pulled any punches.

In one front page story in the *Times* of November 19, 1909, the Colonel referred to his colleague of the *P.-I.* as *"a miscreant"*, *"a scoundrel"*, *"a liar"*, and *"the most contemptible cur who ever sat in an editorial seat in America"*. On the other hand, the Colonel pointed out in the same story, he, Colonel Blethen, had *"a character and standing that 'Erastus Brainerd' and the little clique of cynical, carping whelps which follow him will not obtain in 10,000 years"*. Furthermore, the Colonel wrote, it was well known by all that he, the Colonel, was *"a big-hearted, true-hearted, true friend of suffering humanity, a true friend, an honest man, a patriotic citizen, a lover of home and the protector of the widow and orphan"*. He quoted Seattle's leading Presbyterian divine, the Reverend Doctor Mark A. Matthews, to back up this modest description of himself.

It will be seen that Engineer Thomson had his hands full when his name was added to the list of the Colonel's personal enemies. Although the *Times* had Democratic leanings in politics, having beaten the drums loudly in favor of William Jennings Bryan and free silver, the Colonel's conservatism was growing in direct ratio to his bankroll. The regrading of the hills cost over six million dollars. The park system cost another four million. Add the water system, the sewers, the paved streets, and the Colonel could feel shooting pains in the region of the pocketbook. At first he expressed his annoyance with Thomson in relatively mild terms; *"The people of Seattle have SUFFERED MUCH from the ARROGANCE OF THOMSON"*, he wrote, using bold-faced type with a lavish hand, *"almost as much, in fact, as they have from his UTTER INCOMPETENCE"*.

But when Thomson announced his greatest scheme of all the Colonel literally flipped. In brief, Thomson's plan was this: he was going to build a great masonry sea wall a half mile offshore and reaching from the Duwamish on the south to Smith's Cove on the north. Then he would sluice Beacon Hill and the remains of Jackson and Dearborn Hills into the space between the sea wall and the existing waterfront. The result would be a sweeping esplanade of perfectly level land across the whole front of the city. Three broad boulevards would be projected north and south between Railroad Avenue (Alaska Way) and the bay.

When Thomson admitted that the cost would probably be at least twice that of all the other regrade operations, the Colonel fired the full broadside he reserved for very special occasions. He devoted the whole front page of the *Times* to R. H. Thomson. Half the page carried a highly colored and not very flattering portrait of the engineer. The other half was devoted to a series of sensational charges against him. Boiled down and sifted out, they alleged that the city engineer had promoted the regrade projects as a vast personal graft, approving exorbitant charges by contractors and splitting the profits with them; that he had purchased tracts of property under various aliases and then forced through improvements at public expense to increase the value of his holdings; that, in brief, he had enriched himslf at the expense of long-suffering taxpayers of Seattle, including Colonel Blethen.

The Colonel's all-out attack achieved the desired results. It resulted in libel suits totalling several hundred thousand dollars and, in the long run, Thomson's reputation survived the bruising it had taken, but the splendid dream of a broad level waterfront as a front yard for Seattle died in the muddy waters of charges, counter-charges and recriminations that ensued. R. H. Thomson's crowning achievement was filed with the forgotten dreams.

The city which emerged at the close of the 20th century's first decade was a compromise between men like Thomson, who dreamed of a super-city of surpassing beauty, and the faction at the other extreme who recoiled instinctively from new ideas with the accompanying possibility of new taxes. The compromise wasn't all it might have been, but it was pretty good. In ten years Seattle had more than tripled its population, paved its streets, acquired 2000 acres of parks and playgrounds, reduced the grade of its once almost perpendicular streets to a maximum of five percent, and achieved a skyline which boasted at least one *bona fide* skyscraper; the Alaska Building was a full fourteen stories high.

The arch-enemy, Tacoma, had been left far behind in those ten years, as had every other aspiring city in the Northwest. Seattle was the undisputed metropolis. Tacoma had been out-distanced but not outfought. You were asking for trouble if you called "The Mountain" *Rainier* inside the city limits of Tacoma. It was *Mt. Tacoma,* and you'd better not forget it, for the two brash young cities took their rivalry seriously and saw nothing ludicrous in quarrelling over the name of a mountain that was older than Ararat, and had been there centuries before the first race of man came down out of the trees.

Unable to top Seattle skyscrapers, Tacoma countered by building a huge wooden sign high on the bluff above the city which proclaimed in electrically lighted letters, *"Watch Tacoma Grow".* It looked impressive, particularly from the deck of a Sound steamboat at night, until unknown parties described by the Tacoma newspapers as "dastardly vandals", switched a few bulbs to make the sign read *"Watch Tacoma Crow".*

Nothing could be proved, but Tacoma knew who was responsible. Its feeling toward its neighboring city was portrayed by the cartoonist of the *Ledger,* who frequently did front page drawings of a ravening wolf with dripping fangs. The wolf was labeled "The Seattle Spirit" and it was constantly engaged in cornering helpless little girls, who represented other Washington cities, and robbing them of various juicy civic prizes.

Somewhere along the line the two rival cities matured to the point of no longer brawling over civic slogans, population figures and the names of mountains and both kept right on growing without that stimulation. The *Times* recently ran a series of regular Chamber of Commerce articles about Tacoma, pointing out its many attractions in glowing terms.

If an editor had tried a stunt like that in the hairy-chested Seattle of 1910 the town would probably have had another lynching.

TACOMA, WASHINGTON, MONDAY, JANUARY 18, 1904.

WOLF!

HI GILL, THREE-TIME WINNER

MARK A. MATTHEWS was a lanky, dynamic Presbyterian minister with a mane of hair and flair for words to rival those of even Colonel Blethen. Arriving in Seattle at the turn of the century to take over the First Presbyterian Church, Doctor Matthews soon made his presence felt as the most influential—and controversial—churchman in town. His church became the largest of its denomination in the United States and his sermons were reprinted full length every Monday in the daily papers. He is one of the four Seattleites who have been immortalized by statues in the public parks, the others being Judge Burke, ex-sheriff and ex-Governor John McGraw, and Chief Seattle.

Mark Matthews liked Seattle as a whole; liked it so well that he frequently sounded more like a Chamber of Commerce booster than a Presbyterian divine, but his suggestions along this line were not without merit. "Let's forget petty piques, personal jealousies, prejudices and opinions and rise to the supreme importance of our plain duty—that of advertising the matchless wealth, opportunities, blessings, privileges and glories of this city and section", was the advice of Doctor Matthews.

But when he talked about the blessings and glories of Seattle he meant the respectable part of town—not the region south of Yesler Way. He was convinced that it needed advertising, surely, but not for promotional purposes. "It's time for the decent people of Seattle to stop ignoring the cesspool in our midst and set about to have it removed", he insisted. With the dramatic flair of a true orator, he thundered from his pulpit against evils which had not heretofore been considered subjects for polite discussion: *"Yesler Way was once a skid road down which logs were pushed to Henry Yesler's sawmill on the waterfront. Today it is a skid road down which human souls go sliding to hell!"*.

The district had been there for a long time and it was still paying handsome dividends to respectable citizens who owned its real estate as well as to the active dealers in sin. Doctor Matthews' verbal blasts didn't remove it, but they gave it a new name. Once it had been "Down on the Sawdust", then the "Lava Beds" and the "Tenderloin", but after Matthews' vivid portrayal of skidding souls the old restricted district became "Skid Road", a title which it has kept to this day, and which had spread to similar districts in cities all over America, although outside the Northwest the term has degenerated into "Skid Row", a grievous error which has been perpetuated by motion pictures and television.

With the departure of Mayor Tom Humes from the Seattle political scene, the city was inclined to make another swing of the moral pendulum in the direction pointed out by Doctor Matthews. Humes was followed by another crop of reform mayors, the most notable of whom was William Hickman Moore, who was elected in 1906. Mayor Moore was not a particularly aggressive executive, but he distinguished himself by winning election with the smallest majority in history as well as by his peculiar choice of a Police Chief to back up the edicts of an administration based on purity and good government. His Chief of Police was none other than ex-Detective Charles W. Wappenstein.

This was the same Wappenstein—"Wappy" to almost everybody in Seattle—who had been fired along with Chief Meredith in the fatal police scandal of 1901. At that time the City Council's investigating committee had pulled no punches in its evaluation of his character. "From the evidence C. W. Wappenstein was found unfit to occupy the position of detective or any other position in the police department", the council had reported to Mayor Humes.

The *Post-Intelligencer's* comments had been even more pointed: *"The severing of Wappenstein's connection with the police department is hailed with satisfaction by every honest man in Seattle. It will be fortunate if this marks the end of public transactions with him and his total eclipse in this community. It is a most excellent riddance".*

It amazed everyone, especially the *P. I.,* when Wappy returned from the darkness of his eclipse to shine as a reforming Police Chief who, according to some of the most critical of the spokesmen of purity, provided Seattle with the best police administration in its history.

Wappenstein, who was short, stocky and owly-eyed, was once described by the *Post-Intelligencer* as resembling "a somewhat disreputable walrus", but to a more discerning eye his attributes were those of a chameleon. Wappy was capable of changing hues to conform with the surroundings in which he found himself. If they wanted reform, he'd give it to them until they were sick of it; sick enough to go back to the prescription he and Colonel Blethen had always recommended for Seattle . . . a wide open restricted district within the limits of those few square blocks south of Yesler Way, with rigid enforcement of vice and gambling laws everywhere else.

The results of the cleanup in the Skid Road district were about what Wappenstein and Blethen had expected. Cries of anguish arose from the city's better element as, once again, the red lights were turned off in the restricted district to peep surreptitiously from behind the drawn shades of windows in apartment and residential areas.

It was reported that "dissolute women" were plying their trade in hotels, railway stations and even public parks, while gambling, having gone underground was completely unrestrained. Residents along the cable car lines to Lake Washington complained that rowdy crowds, once pretty well confined to the Skid Road, were flocking to the lakefront parks and throwing whiskey bottles through the windows of unoffending taxpayers along the way.

Wappy padlocked the Leschi Park pavilion when the week-end dances there got completely out of control. It was reported that the pavilion social events not only made the nights hideous with brawling and caterwauling, but were "conducive to the ruin of young women". A housewife residing at 3004 Yesler Way reported that she had been forced to discharge her seventeen-year-old servant girl who had developed a weakness for sneaking out to join the drunken ex-Skid Roaders on the Leschi Park cable cars.

"She was a good girl when I first employed her", the irate lady told police, "but when she started going to Leschi Park she went from bad to worse".

Chief Wappenstein clucked sympathetically as he promised to abate this particular nuisance, but in the privacy of his office he grinned a happy grin under his walrus mustache. Events were proving the truth of his theory on the only practical—and profitable—way to control vice. He suspected that Seattle would soon be ready to turn the lights on again down on the Skid Road.

So did Colonel Blethen.

And so did Councilman Hiram Charles Gill, erstwhile champion of the defrauded Tex Rickard.

Hi Gill was among those especially repugnant to Doctor Matthews. The representative of the Third Ward had risen to president of the City Council, but his law practice hadn't changed much. He still represented many of the Skid Road's more prominent saloon keepers, gambling house operators and parlor house proprietors, and he saw nothing improper in relinquishing the gavel of city government to go down to the court room for the purpose of arranging bail when Wappy's men raided one of his clients' places of business.

This, in the opinion of Mark Matthews, was unethical, improper and bad publicity for Seattle. National magazines were still sending writers to Seattle when they wanted a real lurid article for the edification of their readers, and they made much of a city government which took time out while its president paid the fines of convicted prostitutes.

Gill, however, was known admiringly as "an independ-

nt little cuss" and it was a description in which he took
nbounded pride. He saw no reason to change colors in an
ffort to blend with the lily-white of the current purity
ampaign, for he was smart enough to know that the city
vould soon be tired of it and looking for a champion of the
pen door policy south of Yesler Way. "When the time
omes", said Hi, "I'm just the bird they'll be looking for".

Chief Wappenstein was, in the meantime, becoming the
air-haired boy of Colonel Blethen and the *Times,* who pic-
ured him as a latter day Sir Galahad ridding the city of hid-
ous dragons of corruption. This high regard was partly the
esult of the Colonel's natural instinct to disagree with the
. I., which held that Wappy was one of the top dragons in
lisguise, but it was also prompted somewhat by numerous
ersonal favors done the Colonel by the Chief, among
hem the assignment of a burly and aggressive police officer
amed Jack Marquett as the little publisher's personal
odyguard.

There were two theories as to Blethen's military title;
ne had it that he was born a colonel, the other that an
astern governor had appointed him to his personal staff
vith that rank, but one point was certain; it wasn't a battle-
ield promotion and the guiding genius of the *Times* pre-
erred to do his actual fighting with printer's ink. Officer
Marquett was a big help to the Colonel in keeping things
n that high plane, and in a later era he gained considera-
le fame in his own right as one of Seattle's leading boot-
eggers.

Among those who disagreed with the *Times'* high regard
or the Chief of Police was King County's up and coming
oung deputy prosecuting attorney, George Vanderveer.
Vanderveer had considerable first-hand knowledge of the
kid Road, for the area interested him personally as well as
rofessionally. He liked to walk the garish streets, listening
o the soap-box orators, the gambling house shills and the
oarse-voiced spielers at the basement entrances of the box
ouse variety theaters. Sometimes he found relief for his
xcess energy by engaging in informal slugging matches
vith festive loggers, celebrating sailors or other denizens of
kid Road. Vanderveer liked nothing better than a knock-

down drag out battle, whether physical, legal, verbal . . .
or a combination of all three.

When tips and personal observations led him to the conclusion that Wappy's show of rigid law enforcement wa
largely a strategy to raise the price of protection, Vander
veer waded into the Chief with the same free-handed styl
that he used on his Skid Road forays. Colonel Blethe
leaped to the defense of his pride and joy, while Erastu
Brainerd moved the *P. I.* onto the firing line in support o
the deputy prosecutor. The *Times* had a new villain and th
P. I. a new hero.

Mayor Moore went out of office in 1908 amid smoke o
battle, and with him went Colonel Blethen's paragon of Po
lice Chiefs, Wappy, who complained bitterly that Seattl
didn't appreciate honest law enforcement when it had i

The front page of the *Times,* which was never dull, be
came truly lurid with heavy-type tales of universal depravi
ty resulting from the second eclipse of Wappenstein, bitte
commentaries on the high-handed tactics of George Van
derveer, and stirring predictions of a great world's fair fo
Seattle to be called the Alaska-Yukon-Pacific Exposition

The Exposition, which had been planned as a modes
display of Alaskan products by the Arctic Club and Cham
ber of Commerce, was adopted as a puny infant by Colone
Blethen and nursed to giant stature. When a bond issu
was floated to finance it, the *Times* went all out to back th
drive, threatening to print the names of wealthy citizen
who refused to contribute in a list of shame, front pag
center. It was highly effective and Colonel Blethen had
good deal of justification for his conviction that Seattle'
Alaska-Yukon-Pacific Exposition was his baby.

With equal vigor the Colonel attacked the condition
which he felt were the result of a Wappensteinless polic
force. "OFFENSES AGAINST DECENCY AND LAW"
the *Times* proclaimed in glaring headlines. *"Frank Displa*
of Vice and utter disregard for statutes in City claimed t
be perfectly clean!".

Then, in a black-bordered box were listed in detail th
law violations observed by the *Times* "at midnight Satur
day". They were under two headings, *"Offenses agains*

decency", which included *"open houses of prostitution, street-walkers plying their trade, boisterous crowds drinking in cafes after midnight, and young girls drinking themselves into intoxication in cafes"*.

"Offenses against the law" which had been noted by the *Times* included *"American Cafe selling liquor after midnight, Newport Cafe selling liquor after midnight, American Cafe selling liquor to minors, Newport Cafe selling liquor to minors and proprietors permitting women to frequent their saloons"*.

Readers who wanted more specific information were well taken care of. It was bad enough, said the *Times,* that Skid Road establishments like the Owl Saloon at Third and Washington and the Olympia Saloon at 201 Second Avenue South were going full blast, with *"Rouge bedecked women frequenting them and enticing men patrons to imbibe freely of beer and other concoctions, brazenly and wantonly carrying on their lewd traffic under the eyes of the police"*, but the evil had, as Colonel Blethen had long predicted, spread to previously decent sections of town. The Newport Cafe on Madison Street failed to close at midnight, as the law demanded and it was observed that *"young girls with drink-flushed faces and sparkling eyes raised their voices in boisterous song and consumed quantities of liquor long after midnight"*.

Clear out at Westlake and Pike, a region whose slumbers had previously been disturbed only by the occasional lowing of a cow or passing of an owl streetcar, the American Cafe was found to be jumping. *"Bartenders and scurrying waiters busied themselves dishing out 'booze' to the thirsty men and women who vied with one another in guzzling liquor long after the saloon upstairs above the cafe was closed to the public"*, the *Times* reported with grave concern.

"Policemen paid by the city to suppress vice stand idle outside the Baltimore Hotel and the Owl Saloon while licentiousness and evil are displayed in the interior", the aroused newspaper asserted, ending its expose of Seattle night life with an interesting question: *"What"*, asked the *Times,* *"is the answer?"*

Presumably Colonel Blethen felt that he, at any rate,

knew what the answer was: C. W. Wappenstein for Chief of Police.

One I. Rosenthal, proprietor of the maligned Newport Cafe on Madison Street, took an advertisement in the *Post-Intelligencer* to defend his business methods and, incidentally, to infer that the Colonel was an unabashed liar who was trying to blackmail Rosenthal because he had refused to advertise in the *Times*. Colonel Blethen reproduced the advertisement on the front page of the *Times*, threatening to sue the *P. I.* and Erastus Brainerd for libel for printing it. Then he swore out a warrant and had Rosenthal dragged off to jail. Brainerd observed that Colonel Blethen was skating on thin ice when he started suggesting libel suits, but the warning didn't slow the Colonel down a bit. When Attorney Richard Saxe Jones, defending Rosenthal in court, repeated the advertising shakedown story, the *Times* observed that he had *"uttered the* MOST INFAMOUS FALSEHOOD *which only a contemptible shyster, defending members of the slums, could formulate"*.

The City Council, disturbed by all the commotion, took a determined step in the direction of righteousness. It passed an ordinance forbidding the purchase or sale of cigarettes within the corporate limits of the city.

George Vanderveer was off on a crusade of his own, convicting Seattle milk producers of conspiracy to fix prices and endearing himself to housewives the length and breadth of the city. The female population had not yet regained the right to vote, but Vanderveer, being a married man himself, didn't underrate its influence. He decided to run for prosecuting attorney in the fall elections of 1908. Colonel Blethen made no comment. He was busy finding a spot for Wappenstein as chief of the special police at the Alaska-Yukon-Pacific Exposition.

Things were strangely quiet for a while. The *Times* devoted most of its space to another pitch for William Jennings Bryan and promotion of the Colonel's exposition. The Great Commoner had made a trip to Washington, visiting the Legislature in session at Olympia for the principal purpose, according to *Times* headlines, of urging full support for the Alaska-Yukon-Pacific Exposition, so the two Big Stories went together perfectly.

A brief flurry of excitement was created when two cable cars, one on the Yesler Way line and the other on James Street, lost their grips at exactly the same moment and raced each other down hill on parallel courses but, as on previous occasions, the gripmen stayed aboard to bring things under control at the brink of destruction, although the conductor of the James Street car was reported to have made the agile but cowardly leap to safety; an act for which he was summarily dismissed from the service by the company inspector on duty at the foot of the hill.

Such trivial matters were swept from the front page of the *Times* during the last week of October, for events had been transpiring behind the scenes. Vanderveer had observed the move to place Wappy in charge of Exposition police and he had not failed to note the fact that Colonel Blethen was pointedly laying off him in his campaign for prosecuting attorney. Putting two and two together, he suspected that the Colonel's silence was a form of tacit bribe . . . you stop picking on Wappy and I'll stop picking on you.

Vanderveer's reaction was typical. He submitted his formal protest against Wappenstein's appointment to the Exposition committee, pointing out that Seattle's effort to gain stature in the eyes of the world would not be enhanced if Wappy were to start selling concession space to pickpockets and prostitutes. This, he made it clear, was not an unlikely eventuality, considering the ex-Chief's previous record.

The front page of the *Times* burgeoned suddenly, devoting most of its available space to George Vanderveer. It had suddenly discovered that he was intimidating helpless old men, terrifying innocent women and browbeating everyone unfortunate enough to fall into his clutches. On the Sunday before election day he got the full treatment. One half of the front page was given over to a drawing tinted in shades of hellish red with a maniacal and bug-eyed Vanderveer portrayed as about to beat the daylights out of a gentlemanly old fellow in wing collar and nose-glasses. The drawing was captioned *"The Kind of a Man He Is"*. The remainder of the front page was devoted to a rather vague charge that the Republican nominee for prosecuting attorney had once made a threatening pass at his father-in-law. Mention was made on page two that Vanderveer's sins also included an attempt to block the appointment of C. W. Wappenstein as chief of Exposition police.

The *Post-Intelligencer* sprang back into the fray like an old war horse at the scent of fresh gunpowder. It charged that Colonel Blethen was back at his old tricks, using the *Times* as a blackjack with which to assault his personal enemies; that he hated City Engineer Thomson because that revered public servant had refused to regrade the street in front of the Colonel's house on Highland Drive, that he hated Hi Gill because the *P. I.'s* City Hall reporter had scooped the *Times* on Council doings, and he hated Vanderveer because the prosecutor had revealed the iniquities of Wappenstein.

On the day after election the *Times* emerged from the smoke of political and journalistic battle to announce in triumphant headlines, "VANDERVEER REBUKED". The story under the headlines said that the citizens of Seattle had again demonstrated their level-headedness to the satisfaction of Colonel Blethen by rejecting the monstrous Vanderveer overwhelmingly at the polls. If you read the account closely you learned that the votes of county bumpkins had, unfortunately, been counted too, and the total King County vote had elected Vanderveer prosecuting attorney.

One thing was clear anyway. Trying to run Seattle as a closed town was no good. It caused nothing but trouble. Hi Gill was quick to feel the stirring of the tide and knew it was about to turn. He advised Seattle to face the facts of life; admit that you can't legislate against human nature, and put sin back on the Skid Road where it could be controlled.

This was music to Colonel Blethen's ears, and furthermore he knew just the Chief of Police to run the Skid Road as it should be run. Seattle was ready for another change, the *Times* was willing to let bygones be bygones as far as Hi Gill was concerned and the former councilman from the Third Ward was elected Mayor by a comfortable majority in the spring election of 1910.

No one was greatly surprised when C. W. Wappenstein was appointed Chief of Police, and Wappy was a happy man. The Skid Road was his oyster; an oyster full of pearls, which he knew exactly how to extract.

Calling a conference of the city's gamblers and brothel operators, Wappy mapped their business strategy for them. The old crib houses were refurnished, new and bigger ones were established, roulette wheels and crap tables were dusted off and put in place. When banks hesitated to lend money for such enterprises, Wappy calmed their fears with reassuring telephone calls. The Chief's share in the operation was simple and direct. He was to receive ten dollars per month per girl from the operator of every house of prostitution in Seattle.

The good citizens who had voted to open up the Skid Road were alarmed at the enthusiasm with which the opening transpired, but all might have gone well had Gill been able to keep his promise to clean up the rest of the city. Unfortunately for him, sin continued to overflow from the restricted district, where Wappy's patrolmen were busy making informal census reports on the number of girls upon whom collections were to be made. There were at least five hundred of them there, but Wappy was greedy. Plans were made to establish a supermarket for sin on Beacon Hill, which was to feature a 500-room brothel, undeniably the largest in the world. The promoters had no trouble selling stock to finance the venture and the City Council, which had refused to vacate city streets for a railroad station, obligingly vacated several of them for this interesting enterprise.

Doctor Matthews could almost smell the brimstone wafted up from the nether regions as he shook his mane and pounded his pulpit at the Presbyterian Church. *"Gillism must go!"* was his battle cry, and he backed it up with action, hiring Burns detectives at his own expense to ferret out evidence of graft and corruption. Blethen and Gill re-

acted typically. The Colonel added the Burns Detective
Agency to his list of undesirables and the *Times* scarehead-
ed exposes of Burns, "the professional spy and sneak". The
cocky Hi, asked if he had gone to the church to hear Matthews' indictment of his administration, replied, "Hell no.
I'm a devout old bird and I make it a rule never to go to
places of amusement on Sunday".

The embattled minister checked the reports of his private eyes by prowling the Skid Road to find out for himself
just what was going on. When he found out he began or-
ganizing the ladies of his church to demand a cleanup of
the city or a recall of its mayor.

The *Times* and the Skid Road were vastly entertained by
the comic aspects of the gaunt young Presbyterian minister
on his round of dives and honkytonks, as well as by the
somewhat naive slogan of the feminine recall workers . . .
"Ladies, get out and hustle!".

The ribald humor of the heathen had no effect on Doctor Matthews. When a spell-binding evangelist named Alexander came to town, the good doctor joined forces with
him to stage one of the most sensational parades in Seattle
history. Striding grimly at the head of an army consisting of
thousands of the city's purest and most respectable womanhood, the two crusaders invaded Skid Road. South of Yesler Way the righteous filled the streets and overflowed into
variety theaters, saloons and honkytonks. The habitues of
the restricted district were shocked, but the respectable ladies had a wonderful time. Most of them had always wanted to see what was going on down there.

Gill was so unconcerned about all the foolishness that he
embarked on the yacht *Rainier*, a luxurious craft built to
the specifications of a local brewer, and took a comfortable
cruise to Alaska. Wappy had just departed on a ten-day
leave of absence to enroll his son in a California military
academy. City Council President Murphy was out of town
too, and that made Max Wardell of the Fourteenth Ward
Acting Mayor.

The Acting Mayor ordered a City Council investigation
of vice, gambling and police corruption. The committee

was headed, fittingly enough, by the Council's vice president.

The results of this probe were reported by the newspapers with some variations. According to the *P. I.*, which Colonel Blethen referred to, when he could bring himself to mention it at all, as the *"Morning Prevaricator"*, the *"Puny Imitator"* and the *"Public Irresponsible"*, things were in a very distressing state indeed. The Seattle *Star* agreed with the *P. I.* and was properly put in its place by the Colonel, who christened it the *"Guttersnipe"*. The *Times* maintained until the bitter end that Mayor Gill's administration had triumphed over its enemies and Chief Wappenstein had received vindication through the Council's investigation.

Apparently forgetting its recent accounts of lurid sin during Wappy's absence from the chieftainship, the *Times* also claimed bitterly that the *Post-Intelligencer* was giving Seattle a bad name by its accounts of lurid sin now that Wappy was back.

"For seven weeks", the outraged Colonel wrote, bearing down hard on the boldfaced type, *"the P. I. has done all that lay in its power to* BLACKEN THE NAME OF SEATTLE, *by exploiting* SLANDER, DEFAMATION *of* CHARACTER *and* ABSOLUTE FALSEHOOD *concerning public officials of this city. The thing has gone so far that* HUNDREDS OF PEOPLE, *recently residents of Seattle, have received letters and telegrams from their eastern friends, either to ascertain the truth, or to beg them to return, rather than take a chance of complete destruction in a city whose crimes compare only with Sodom and Gomorrah"*.

As a clincher, the Colonel unlimbered his heavy artillery which was used only in times of grave crisis—the whole front page of the Sunday *Times*.

A gruesome spectacle was unfolded over their breakfast coffee by Seattle citizens on the morning of October 23, 1910. The upper two thirds of the *Times* portrayed a fanged thug in a black burglar's mask beating the life from a prone victim. The brutish attacker was labelled *Wilson*

—The *Post-Intelligencer's* publisher—and the gnarled club with which he was belaboring his victim was marked *Newspaper*. The prostrate figure which, except for the walrus mustache, was a dead ringer for Sir Galahad, was labelled *Wappenstein*. Crimson blood poured from the victim's skull, which was badly cracked, and flowed downward toward the heavy type which filled the page's lower third. Behind a lighted window sat an unsuspecting figure. It was in silhouette and it wasn't labelled, but everyone knew who the *Times* artist meant. The figure was smoking a corncob pipe.

This frightening work of art was captioned "WILSON'S DREAM" with the subtitle, *"First One . . . Then the Other"*. The Colonel then demonstrated that Erastus Brainerd of the *P. I.* wasn't the only newspaperman in Seattle with a classical education. He quoted Virgil on *Slander*, and Shakespeare's *"He that filches from me my good name robs me that which not enriches him and makes me poor indeed"*.

Thus well warmed up, he continued in his own inimitable prose: *"Former Senator Wilson can not control Mayor Hiram C. Gill, nor can he control Chief of Police Charles W. Wappenstein. He can not name Gill's appointees to municipal offices. He can not make Gill a contributing member of the Post-Intelligencer's news staff. He can not force Gill to construct a political machine for the newspaper proprietor's benefit.*

"Former Senator Wilson can not dictate the conduct of police affairs. He can not control the Tenderloin or its denizens by the aid of Wappenstein's police department. He can not make the policemen of Seattle reporters for his newspaper.

"But all these things he has tried to do . . . and much more. He has failed. Mayor Gill will not kneel in the dust. Chief Wappenstein will not kiss the royal feet.

"This is crime. No punishment can be too great for such offenders. Moreover, Gill and Wappenstein are both poor —both in debt. Both occupy public office—therefore Wilson's newspaper, supplied with low cunning and desperate craft by Brainerd, may be used to destroy them.

"Nothing is wrong with either of them—but Wilson must have revenge! Wappenstein must be deprived of reputation, friends, his living wage! Gill's present and future must be blasted—His children disgraced! Why? BECAUSE THESE TWO MEN WILL NOT CALL SENATOR WILSON 'MASTER'!"

Doctor Matthews and his Forces of Decency remained unmoved by even this rolling barrage of art, literature and red ink. The movement to recall Hi Gill from office went on unchecked.

Hi was no shrinking violet, and he issued pungent comments of his own, which the *Times* tidied up here and there and then printed in great detail.

The Forces of Decency were flocking to the standard of a new reform candidate selected by the righteous to replace Gill. The first choice of purity was a politically inexperienced real estate dealer named George Dilling, whom Gill dismissed scornfully as having less brains than an underfed microbe. Hi admitted that Dilling, having avoided politics, had practically no enemies, but, said Hi, "His friends can't stand him".

Senator Wilson of the *Post-Intelligencer* fared little better in the character analysis made of him by Seattle's mayor—"a disgruntled, dyspeptic reformed cigarette fiend". "They seem to think up there", said Hi, "that they can write an editorial yelling for the Police Chief's head and that I'll bring it in on a silver platter in time for the next edition. Well, they picked the wrong bird". Hi's dander was up and he further alienated the hustling ladies of decency as "a bunch of magpies".[1]

The City Council's special prosecutor, J. Y. C. Kellogg also received attention from the embattled defenders of the Mayor's office. The *Times* quoted bawdy house proprietors

---

[1] It was twenty years before another Seattle mayor, Johnny Dore, succeeded in riling up as many high-minded ladies as did Hi when he made that statement. Dore referred to his fair critics as "fur-clad hussies".

who claimed that Kellogg had, as soon as his Skid Road investigation began, *"repudiated his wine and other bills, declaring that, as a member of the City Council, he was entitled to entertainment and considered himself merely a guest"*.

Plans for the giant red light district on Beacon Hill were snowed under in the controversy and the sprawling building might have been forgotten in its role of innocent apartment house, had not an Air Force bomber from Boeing Field crashed into it in 1951.

Before the recall petitions were filed the ladies got back the right to vote which had been taken from them back in 1887. They gave their supoprt to purity, just as they had a quarter of a century before; most of them did at any rate. The five hundred carefully counted damsels of the Skid Road had long since abandoned morality and they voted their convictions, but their support wasn't enough. When the votes were counted in February of 1911 Hiram Gill was out, less than a year after his election, and Dilling was in.

Sadness and depression settled on the Skid Road as a grand jury returned indictments against Wappenstein and two of his most prominent business associates, Clarence Gerald and Gideon Tupper. Even uptown Seattle was stirred when the same jury indicted Colonel Alden J. Blethen. It was charged that he was part owner of a building which housed a gambling layout.

The Colonel beat the rap without even having to appear on the stand, but poor Wappy went to the state penitentiary at Walla Walla, where he probably suffered more than his partners in crime, for a policeman's lot is truly not a happy one when he's in prison.[2]

As for jaunty Hi Gill, he tried for vindication, again on the open town ticket, in 1912. He lost to George Cotterill, a mildly liberal reform candidate who had once been assist-

---

[2] Just before Christmas, 1913, Wappy was granted a conditional pardon by Governor Ernest Lister. It was issued at the recommendation of Doctor Mark Matthews and the condition was that Wappy would agree never again to show his face in the city of Seattle. As far as is known, he never did.

ant city engineer under Colonel Blethen's arch-enemy, R. H. Thomson.

Then Hi saw the light. In 1914 he announced that he had got religion. He wanted to be elected Mayor so he could make up for his past sins and make his grandchildren proud of him. Seattle was snuffling audibly as it hurried to the polls to give Little Old Hi another chance.

Gill's second term coincided with the advent of state prohibition, and the Mayor delighted Doctor Matthews and the Forces of Decency by personally leading the police on liquor raids. He smashed kegs and bottles with the abandon of a Carrie Nation, and citizens were frequently awakened in the dead of night by prohibitionist policemen who searched their rooms, dumped their bedding on the floor and dragged them off to jail if any liquor was found on the premises. If none was found the law departed without explanation or apology.

The cynical held that Hi Gill was using Wappy's old psychology . . . ramming law and order down the public's throat until it was good and sick of it. The old line-up was completely reversed. Doctor Matthews was among Gill's most loyal admirers. Colonel Blethen and the *Times* lambasted the Mayor unmercifully. The people re-elected him in 1916, a humiliation which Colonel Blethen was spared. The peppery old genius of the *Times* died in 1915.

Gill's third term was a mess. Another Chief of Police was shot out from under him by a grand jury and there was more talk of recall. Mark Matthews stood by the Mayor, who claimed he was doing the best he could, but the United States government took a hand to finish him off politically. The Skid Road was wide open again and it was spreading venereal disease through the ranks of Northwest-based Army units at an alarming rate. Seattle was thoroughly shocked when the armed forces placed the whole city off-limits to all military personnel.

Hi Gill tried to reform himself and the city once more, but it was too late. After the election of 1918 Hi Gill was a political corpse and the big office at City Hall was occupied by an impeccable reformer named Ole Hanson. Doctor Matthews left the Skid Road to its own devices, preferring to spend his leisure cruising Lake Washington in his yacht. It was relaxing for the Doctor, but disturbing to Foreman Adrian Gallaher of the Lake Washington Park district, who recalls that he received frequent summonses from the evangelical yacht during the summer months. Young couples from the University were in the habit of stopping off from canoe rides at Foster Island for a bit of swimming, frequently without benefit of bathing suits. When Doctor Matthews spied such antics he would notify Foreman Gallaher, who would then sneak up on the young bathers in a police car with open cut-out and screeching siren. Since Lake Washington Boulevard was even more narrow and winding then than it is now the sinners had ample warning, with the result that, as Gallaher says happily, "we never did manage to catch any of them, but we put on a wonderful show for Doc Matthews".

Hi Gill may not have completely established the faith of his grandchildren in his political career and personal integrity, but he found a niche in history with Honest Tom Humes; they were the only mayors of Seattle to ever receive three terms in office. It seems as if that ought to prove *something*.

SHAPE OF THINGS TO COME

THE SEATTLE of 1915 was, from an objective viewpoint, essentially the city that we know today. The pattern of the future had been cut and the young metropolis was fitting itself to it solidly. A present-day Seattleite, projected backward in time, might have to look twice to identify his hometown as it was in 1910, but he would have no trouble recognizing the 1915 version of the city.

The big regrade had been practically completed. The skyline to the north was no longer dominated by the Victorian towers of the old Washington Hotel at the top of Denny Hill. The hill was gone and a new Washington Hotel had already been built on level ground at that historic location. The Territorial University has been replaced by the first modern office buildings of the "Metropolitan District", and only the five graceful white columns of the ancient structure remained—re-erected on a new University campus bordering Lake Union.[1]

---

[1] Professor Edmund Meany was instrumental in having many of the Alaska-Yukon-Pacific Exposition buildings converted to university use, the exposition having been held on the new University campus. It was Meany, too, who had the columns of the Territorial University re-erected on the new campus, a ceremony which was performed by the Class of 1911.

The original ten acre plot donated to the school by Arthur Denny was already valued in millions of dollars and was producing a handsome revenue to help erect the new pseudo-Gothic university buildings on the lake shore.

The city's southern landmark then, as now, was the white, many-windowed Smith Tower with its triangle-roofed tower a full forty-two stories above Second Avenue. It had been a proud day for Seattle in October of 1910 when plans for the new building were released by L. C. Smith, the typewriter king. The *Times* published a colored drawing of the proposed skyscraper almost the full height of the front page, accompanying it with a jubilant announcement, *"Seattle to get tallest structure outside of New York to rear immense tower 42 stories above the street"*. The story led off with a sentence of such remarkable length that it did full justice to the dimensions of the building it was describing:

"Forty-two stories high, the tallest building in the United States outside of New York and the third highest mercantile building in the world in linear feet, with a huge glass ball inclosing an electric flash light surmounting its tower at a height of 467 feet from the street level, with glistening walls of cream colored brick on the main building and pure white tiling on the exterior of its twenty-two story tower, the magnificent L. C. Smith Building, to be erected at the northeast corner of Second Avenue and Yesler Way, at an estimated cost of $1,500,000, will make Seattle remarkable all over the country in the matter of commercial buildings and furnish the city with a landmark that will fix itself upon the memory of visitors from all over the United States".

The *Times* would have been well justified in pausing for breath after that one, but it didn't. There was other joyful news to be announced on the same front page. The 1910 census returns had just come in, giving Seattle an official 241,500 and Tacoma 82,972. This cheering word was bannered above the soaring tower of the Smith Building, with the added tidings that Tacoma had been caught trying to pad its census count. *"City of Destiny, caught with goods, has 33,296 names cut from padded rolls showing 116,268"*, the *Times* chortled gleefully.

By 1915 the "electric flash light" in the tower was projecting its rays above the city, although a few cynics, who had counted them, claimed there *weren't* 42 stories between light and street, and the population had grown to three hundred thousand. The visitor who came to town by rail would probably emerge from the high-towered Union Station on King Street, which was a far cry from the wooden shanty that had served as terminus for the rusty orphan line to Stuck Junction. Across the way at City Hall Park things looked much as they do today. The imposing bulk of the ten-story Frye Hotel to the left, then the triangle of green called Prefontaine Place, named for the pioneer priest who had built the city's first Catholic church with his own hands, then the soaring white column of the Smith Building and the double-winged City Hall, although that building was only half as tall as it is today. County offices were still housed in the old courthouse on "Profanity Hill", high above the city center at Eighth and Alder.

Walking down Yesler's old skid road toward the waterfront, a glance to the right at the base of the Smith Building would reveal what Seattle was proudly calling "the Second Avenue Canyon", lined with tall buildings all the way to the New Washington Hotel. Ten years earlier the city had been waiting for the Alaska Building to be completed so that it could boast a fourteen-story skyscraper.

Double car tracks carried a diminishing line of orange trolley cars into the distance to the north, while the half-open and half-windowed cable cars clanked through at right angles on Yesler, Madison and James. A surprising number of automobiles, followers of the pioneer Woods Electric of 1900, would be parked along the curbs or chugging up and down the paved thoroughfare; black, leather-upholstered touring cars mostly, with a sprinkling of bright red sports roadsters, brass-bound, high-wheeled Fords and sedately gliding electric cabriolets with equally sedate ladies at the helm.

Moving on to Pioneer Place, which is the cradle of the

city, the visitor would then, as now, reach a shabby fairyland where time seems to have stood still. The maze of streetcar tracks is gone now, along with the medley of whistle-blasts from the myriad little steamboats of the Mosquito Fleet scurrying in and out of the landing places at Colman Dock. Aside from that, it is almost the same at Pioneer Place today as it was forty years ago; the busy pigeons and the idle men from the Skid Road, the narrow, blank windows of the old ornate brick buildings that were the first to rise from the ashes of the Great Fire, the cast-iron gingerbread and arched roof of the public comfort station . . . and the garish colors of the Totem Pole.

The Totem came to Seattle in the hold of the steamship *City of Seattle,* chartered by the *Post-Intelligencer* and the jubilant Chamber of Commerce to carry an excursion party to Alaska in 1899. The chamber members wanted to see for themselves the source of the golden harvest that was flowing across the Seattle docks. On the way back the party stopped off at Tongass Island to pick up a few souvenirs, among them a fifty-foot totem pole carved by Tlingit Indians. When the party got back in town there was some discussion as to what should be done with this rather unwieldy trophy. Since nobody could think of anything else to do with a fifty-foot totem pole, it was decided to present it to the city. The City Council, delighted at getting something for nothing, even a totem pole, accepted it with thanks.

Pioneer Place, officially a city park, was selected as the site for its erection and public unveiling. The *P. I.,* as co-sponsor of the excursion which had brought back the pole, played this civic project up enthusiastically. The *Times* viewed the proceedings sourly. When the pole was ready for its official dedication on October 18, 1899, the *Post-Intelligencer* crowed happily: *"Let critics cavil, and envious little journals advertise their sour grapes, Seattle now has a chance to judge for itself as to the merits, artistic and otherwise, of the justly celebrated Totem Pole".*

The next day the *P. I.* was moved to poesy in reporting the gala unveiling of the "wonderful object, fantastically carved and painted", further describing it as

*"A rude, strong piece of sculpture,
carved by a savage, but steady hand—
The shadow of the wilderness in its
deep, rugged lines".*

Whether the *Times* liked it or not, the unveiling of the
Totem Pole was the biggest thing in town that day. A
crowd, described by the *P. I.* as tremendous, had filled the
streets around Pioneer Place by the time the delegation
from the Chamber of Commerce arrived. Chairman J. W.
Clise of the Totem Pole Committee mounted the rostrum
and introduced Attorney Will H. Thomson, who made a
"brief, but witty and stirring" presentation speech. Major
W. V. Rhinehart accepted the Totem on behalf of the city,
making his opening remarks in the Chinook Jargon, a
touch which evoked great laughter from the crowd, as did
the Major's sly inference that, the Totem having been acquired by a group which contained a lot of lawyers, there
might be some question as to whether or not the original
Indian owners had been cheated out of it.

Then a box containing newspapers, documents and other
historic material, including a badge of the W.C.T.U., which
was holding its national convention in Seattle, was sealed
into the Totem's concrete base. Apparently these interesting
relics were subsequently forgotten and are still there, sealed
up safely under the paving of Pioneer Place.

Finally, a workman jerked a cord and the wrappings fell
from the "wonderful object", revealing figures which the
Post-Intelligencer described as, from bottom to top, a rav-
en, a grampus, an eagle, a black bear, a frog, a red man
and a kingfisher, all of them looking so good-natured "that
a smile of sympathy is forced from every beholder, from
sheer sympathy".[2]

The *P. I.* guessed wrong on five out of seven of the totemic figures and it also gave a somewhat garbled version
of the legend they were supposed to convey. Like all good

---

[2] Four decades later, when an "exact duplicate" of the old Pole
was unveiled, the *P. I.* reversed itself, referring to it as "Sixty feet
of freshly-carved monsters ferocious enough to set a lady tourist
tittupy with horror."

totems, this one *did* tell a story, but one fact which its carvers hadn't made clear was that this pole was the personal property of the Tlingit tribe. It remained for a delegation of the Indians themselves to do that. They came to town indicating that they were pretty near mad enough to reenact the Battle of Seattle.

The *P. I.* charged that the Tlingits had been put up to it by totem-chasing lawyers, but the government backed the claim of the original owners. Eight members of the Totem Pole Committee were arrested and fined $500 each. The *Times* was delighted, as were Seattle's rivals among the cities of the Northwest . . . especially Tacoma.

This, they said, was a fine example of the wolfish "Seattle Spirit", which had long been gobbling up universities, industries, custom houses and mountains of the State of Washington.

Now it was ravening across the borders of a friendly power!

Seattle made a fast deal with the troublesome Tlingits, who had the satisfaction of carrying a bit of Alaska gold north from Seattle for a change.

The original pole stayed in place until 1938, when some unknown scoundrel set it afire. The outside wasn't badly singed, but when Bill Hall, the city park department's totem pole surgeon, climbed a swaying fire ladder to make a diagnosis, he reported critical internal injuries.

Like most of the antique totems, this one had been carved from a big cedar log, then hollowed out behind to form a sort of long half-cylinder. Before its installation at Pioneer Place it had been built up with wood and metal backing to make it look like a solid pole again. The fire had eaten its way upward between pole and backing, weakening it so badly that it would have to come down.

Down it came, to be hauled away by a city light truck and suffer the indignity of being stored in a warehouse with worn-out electric poles. The concrete base, still containing the forgotten relics of Old Seattle, was covered with dirt and further hidden with a layer of paving.

The Totem was gone, but not forgotten. Pioneer Place looked naked and desolate. Tourists complained bitterly.

In the end, a bereaved Seattle demanded an exact duplicate of the original pole for Pioneer Place, an assignment which was carried out with the cooperation of many agencies, including the Alaska Steamship Company and the United States Forest Service. The crumbling old totem was shipped back to serve as a model for the new one, which was carved by descendants of the original Tlingit craftsmen. Actually, the new pole is more authentic than the old one, for it is painted in proper colors. The original was so besmeared with gaudy paint, applied at the whim of non-Indian craftsmen, that its creators would have had difficulty in recognizing it.

Forty years ago, as today, Seattle had its quota of picturesque characters who weren't carved on totem poles, and a fair share of them were to be encountered in the vicinity of Pioneer Place. One who was particularly noteworthy was a portly old gentleman with a luxurious white beard and an ingenious headgear in the form of a small umbrella.

The "Umbrella Man" was something of a celebrity in his own right, but he became almost as much a tradition as the Totem Pole when the *Times'* cartoonist, "Dok" Hager borrowed his likeness to adorn the daily weather reports on that paper's front page. The old gentleman was portrayed with a flag projecting jauntily from his umbrella hat, the flag bearing such timely symbols as a rayed sun, cryptic warnings of *$H2O$ or SnO,* or occasional outbursts of *"Glorious", "Real Summery"* or, at the opposite extreme, *"Awful".*

The Umbrella Man in the *Times* cartoon version conversed slangily with a spritely little duck who also wore an umbrella hat and was known as "The Kid". The two discussed the favorite topics of the day, and always with beaming good humor. No matter how vitriolic the battles might rage throughout the rest of the *Times,* there was never anything but gentle humor in the corner sacred to the Umbrella Man and his web-footed companion.

The Umbrella Man was almost a trademark of the *Times* for two decades, becoming so popular that plaster statuettes and picture postcards of him sold like flapjacks and thousands of subscribers ordered monthly calendars featuring the old man and his duck. He continued to present the weather report many years after the original flesh and blood Umbrella Man was gone from his old haunts and most later generation Seattleites were unaware that he had ever really existed.

The original Umbrella Man was one Robert E. Patton, who arrived spectacularly in Seattle in the summer of 1900, striding erect and barrel-chested from the railroad station to the Horseshoe Saloon, where he announced that despite the fact that he was ninety years old he felt confident that he could whip any man in the house at boxing, catch-as-catch-can wrestling or pin pool.

Since there was no merit to be gained in physical combat with a ninety-year-old gentleman wearing an umbrella, the challenge was accepted by the saloon's top pool expert. The house man got in one good shot, after which Patton took over the cue and won two games without giving his opponent a chance at another shot.

After that the old fellow took up his abode in a houseboat on Lake Union, where he spent the mornings fishing for perch. Afternoons he was in the habit of strolling downtown to putter about lending a helping hand wherever he felt it was needed and sometimes settling down on a Pioneer Place bench to brag a little about his war record if he could find a suitable listener. He claimed to have seen service in the Mexican, Black Hawk and Civil Wars and he did collect a pension for wounds received at the Battle of Antietem.

At the age of 95 the Umbrella Man came upon a burly teamster beating an overloaded horse which was bogged down on an unpaved hillside street. The old gentleman beat the daylights out of the teamster, to the intense delight of a large circle of onlookers and, presumably, the abused horse.

The advent of the automobile was the Umbrella Man's downfall. He had been in the habit of obligingly lifting mired wagons to solid footing when he came upon them in the streets, so when he spied his first bogged-down horseless carriage he hurried across the street to render the same service. His failure to budge the cumbersome touring car so

humiliated him that he left town soon afterward to spend
the rest of his days comfortably in a Southern California
soldiers' home, supported by his pension and the additional
payment given him by the *Times* for the use of his likeness
on the weather reports. History does not record whether
the old fellow discarded his legendary umbrella hat when
he reached Southern California.

There were other characters in Pioneer Place in those
days too, not all of them as benignly helpful as the Umbrella Man. Some of them stood on soap boxes to make fighting speeches which were listened to by hard-bitten men in
stagged pants and logger's boots and the faded dungarees
of migratory farm workers or sailors from the coastal lumber fleet. The Skid Road, with its cheap restaurants and
rooming houses, was their stopping place between jobs and
Pioneer Place was their counsel ground.

The soap box orators asked disturbing questions of their
listeners. They pointed out the skyscrapers, the luxurious
hotels, the glittering stores of the mushrooming city, and
they asked the working men in Pioneer Place if they know
who, by rights, owned them.

Their listeners shifted their tobacco-cuds and scraped
the cobblestones with their spiked boots; "Yah", they knew
who owned them. "Them millionaires uptown".

"And who", the orators shouted, *"had made those millions—the timber millions, the coal millions, the salmon
millions. Not a handful of portly old gentlemen uptown at
the Rainier Club, surely. No, by God; those millions had
been made with the sweat and blood of you poor, dumb
working stiffs. Made in the highball logging camps where a
man's life's cheaper than beans in the company store.
Made in the shingle mills where the weavers are through
after ten years because after that they don't have any fin-
gers left on their hands. Made in the coal mines where the
miners never see a minute of God's daylight from September to June and the rotten mine-props aren't replaced until
after the top falls in. You made it—YOU!—and what
share of it are you getting?"*

The listeners stirred uneasily and scratched their heads.
Come to think of it, they weren't getting much; a spot in a

verminous bunk-house or foc'sl to throw their own greasy blankets; hard, dangerous work from dawn to dark at wages that didn't provide much future outside the county poor farm—if they were lucky enough to get in.

There was uneasy stirring uptown too, at the sedate clubs where the millionaires, actual and prospective, gathered; at City Hall and in the editorial rooms of the newspapers. At first the city's very wealthy minority at one extreme and the unwashed drifters of the Skid Road's fringes at the other extreme were the only people much concerned with the soap box anarchy of Pioneer Place. The drifters signed up for red membership cards in an organization they called the Industrial Workers of the World and they began to talk radical nonsense about ten hour working days and logging camps with clean bedding. At the uptown clubs the cheroots glowed angry red and the talk there was of creeping socialism and it's time to call a halt, by God!

Sometimes the police charged in to drag away an especially troublesome orator, but the Skid Road audiences were more frequently inclined to interfere as the ranks of the red card holders grew. Sometimes the sailors and loggers waded in to liberate their articulate brother. On one such occasion a half dozen helmeted cops were counted laid out in the gutter when newspapermen came down to view the aftermath.

Seattle's middle class, not having as much to lose as the very wealthy or as much to gain as the very poor, were interested in other things.

A Seattle high school football team took on a Chicago squad for the championship of the United States and the population of the city risked life and limb riding the roofs of cable cars to Madison Park where the game was played. According to newspaper accounts, even "the favored rich came out in automobiles", most of which got hopelessly bogged down in the gooey mud churned up by the feet of tens of thousands of rooters. Doctor Matthews stomped the mud into flying spray when Seattle fell behind and lifted his voice in prayer when his team rallied to forge ahead. An excited father dashed through the quagmire to run interference for his son and had to be dragged away by the police. Seattle won the championship of the United States.

A whale had stranded at Alki Point and a brisk southwest breeze informed Seattle and all its environs that the whale was in a distressingly moribund condition. Angry groups on street corners discussed the probability of Tacoma interests having towed it there on purpose.

Down on the waterfront the Alaska liner *Alameda* charged Colman Dock and set a new record by sailing completely through the waiting room, which was full of people, and sinking the stern-wheeler *Telegraph* tied up at the opposite side. No one was hurt, except the *Alameda's* engineer, who lost his job and his ticket.

There was the Alaska-Yukon-Pacific Exposition, which turned out to be all Colonel Blethen had hoped it would be, and was policed in a highly creditable manner by the special guards of C. W. Wappenstein.

Judge Burke and John McGraw and R. H. Thomson had pushed through some action at last on the ship canal that had been proposed by Uncle Tom Mercer on the Fourth of July of 1854 and which had been started by Harvey Pike with a shovel and wheelbarrow. The government had taken over the project and although there were a few setbacks—on one occasion a retaining dam broke to spill ten feet of water out of Lake Union into the bay, knocking down the Fremont Bridge and standing all the houseboats in the lake on end—it was just as good as accomplished.[3]

And after the profitable civic merriment of the Exposition there were yearly festivals every summer to look forward to. A contest was held to pick a name for them and a teacher at John B. Allen School suggested an Indian word, *Potlatch*. It was adopted and a *Times* artist named E. F. Brotze was inspired by the Pioneer Place Totem Pole to

---

[3] An earlier canal project, begun in 1901 and abandoned in 1907, would have connected Lake Washington directly with Puget Sound by means of a cut through Beacon Hill. This accomplished little except to arouse an argument which probably delayed construction of the canal on its present site for a number of years.

design a symbol for the big Seattle carnival. It was called the Potlatch Bug and you were expected to wear one during Potlatch Week, if you knew what was good for you.

There were plenty of exciting things to talk about and to look at without going down Yesler Way to listen to soap box prophets on the Skid Road. Seattle was in the last flurries of growing up and the rumbling down there was just one symptom of it.

The Potlatch was more fun and it was the Potlatch that provided the scene for the final violent explosion which Seattle had to get out of its system before it reached maturity.

CITY GROWN UP

THE FABULOUS Alaska-Yukon-Pacific Exposition had convinced Seattle that a well-staged community festival could be profitable as well as enjoyable. The Potlatch celebration was the natural outgrowth of that conviction.

Miss Pearl Dartt, who suggested the winning title for the annual summer carnival, borrowed the term *Potlatch* from the Chinook Indian jargon. According to George Shaw, who compiled a dictionary of that primitive trade language, Potlatch meant "*A present or gift; expecting no return; a donation. The Potlatch was the greatest institution of the Indian . . . From far and near assembled the invited guests and tribes and with feasting, singing, chanting and dancing, the bounteous collection was distributed: a chief was made penniless, the wealth of a lifetime was dissipated in an hour, but his head ever after was crowned with the glory of a satisfied ambition; he had won the reverence and honor of his people. It was a beautiful custom; beautiful in the eyes of the natives of high or low degree*".

A typical Indian Potlatch was staged by Chief John Seattle at his farm near Auburn in the spring of 1907. It was a "Sad Potlatch", given in memory of his son Matthew, a youthful orator of great renown, who had died during his senior year in a Kansas law school. That being the case, the singing and dancing were abandoned, but the basic concept of the Potlatch was carried out. The old chief, sadly aged and grief-stricken by the death of his son, who had been the pride of all the Puget Sound Indians, distributed two thousand dollars in gold to the guests at his party. It was every cent the old chief had, but by his standards it was the only proper gesture to be made in memory of his son.

The standards of white Seattle weren't exactly the same. As Colonel Blethen pointed out in the *Times,* "*When an Indian gives a Potlatch he has a purpose in it*". It was made clear that Seattle's purpose was to attract as many temporary guests as possible with the highly practical hope that a lot of their dollars would stay in town permanently. This was one point upon which the daily press agreed. "*No one expects the citizens of Seattle to strip themselves to their overalls, as is the Indian custom*", the *P. I.* assured its readers before the first Potlatch opened in the summer of 1911. As far as is known, no citizen of Seattle did; not permanently or voluntarily at any rate.

The exuberant spirits of a youthful giant went into the Golden Potlatch of 1911. The businessmen of the city organized three bands of *Tilikums* called *Ikt, Mokt,* and *Klone* (One, Two, Three in Chinook). Combined, they formed the *Tilikums of Elttaes,* a sort of primitive Greater Seattle Inc., dedicated to publicity and promotion for the city, but with heavy emphasis on having a hell of a good time in the process.

Bands of *Tilikums* invaded the sacred precincts of Tacoma to plaster huge Potlatch Bugs on store windows, streetcars, public buildings and even the Tacoma Totem Pole, which that city had been claiming was taller than the *real* Totem Pole at Pioneer Place.

The rage and indignation of Tacomans was so satisfying that *Ikts, Mokts* and *Klones* extended their rough and ready publicity tactics as far as Portland, a staid and dignified city which was accustomed to sniff haughtily at Seattle's bumptious doings. Outraged at being plastered with Seattle Potlatch Bugs, Portland jailed happy *Tilikums* in large batches, but as fast as they were jailed more loyal tribesmen came down from Seattle to bail them out.[1]

Some of the old Potlatch stunts have survived to the effete days of Seattle's Hollywoodized Seafair of today, but they are performed with less gusto and originality nowadays. Take the ritualistic kidnapping of the Mayor, for instance.

In 1955 West Seattle "Indians" snatched Mayor Allan Pomeroy from his office and dragged him to Pioneer Place, where he was tied fast to the Totem Pole with many lengths of clothesline, an item which has historical significance in Seattle since the one owned by Mary Denny was purloined to make the first sounding of the harbor.

After that, however, things reached a sort of anti-climax, with Seafair Indians looking self-consciously fierce for the benefit of TV cameramen and the Mayor knowing all along that he was perfectly safe, unless somebody picked that particular moment to set the Totem Pole on fire again. (He did complain afterward that a small Indian boy had carried realism to the point of kicking him rather painfully on the shins, and that the beak of Grandfather Raven had left black and blue marks between his shoulder-blades, but it was all perfectly harmless and everyone knew it.)

Back in 1912 they kidnapped Mayor George Cotterill, who had been elected to office after Hi Gill's first upset and the brief tenure of reformer George Dilling. Mayor Cotterill was also conducted to Pioneer Place where he was lashed to the original Totem Pole. It was then that the true originality of the pioneer was displayed. A muscular *Tilikum* stepped back fifty paces from the helpless Mayor and took careful aim at him with a wicked-looking and strictly authentic carving knife. The bronzed arm whipped out in a blur of motion, at which precise moment another of the brotherhood released the spring on an ingenious device

---

[1] One of the Tilikums' more serious projects was the erection of the fine bronze statue of Chief Seattle at "Tilikum Place", Fifth and Denny Way. The statue, designed by Sculptor James Wehn, was authorized by the City Council in 1907, but it took the determined *Tilikums of Elttaes* to pry out the funds for its actual unveiling in 1912.

which jabbed the Mayor in the spine with just enough force to convince him that the flung knife had tranfixed him and gone out behind. Mayor Cotterill almost ushered in Potlatch Days with a heart attack.

Years afterward an old-timer reminisced admiringly, "That gadget merely touched him, but I'll never forget the yell he let out as long as I live".

Thus lustily was ushered in the Seattle Potlatch. Scarlet and yellow Potlatch Bugs were hawked on the streets, and ownership of one entitled you to cast a vote for the festival king, or *Hyas Tyee*, for it was a man's world in those days and the only queen in evidence was a huge Miss Seattle of paper mache seated on a float and holding aloft a cornucopia of plenty and a model of the gold ship *Portland*.

Seattle's history and traditions furnished the background for the carnival, with characters portrayed who really meant something to the city. The *Portland* had met the usual fate of Alaska liners a few years earlier and was rusting away on a northern reef, but another old Nome liner, the *Utopia*, was dressed up to look like the original treasure ship. Steaming in to Schwabacher's Wharf, she disgorged a carnival crew which included King Gold, Peter Puget, Soapy Smith (the villain), and numerous Oriental characters presumably left over from the Exposition.

A grand parade was held on Second Avenue, featuring sixteen floats which cost the fabulous sum of sixteen thousand dollars. There were scores of chugging automobiles bedecked with flowers and carrying the "favored rich" in all their finery. The horseless carriages often broke down, making the parade's progress erratic, but the all-male cast was thankful for the pauses. It was hot, and high silk hats, prince alberts and celluloid collars made heavy going.

Street light standards were converted into gaudy totem poles. There were fast speed-boat races on Lake Washington, dancing on the streets presided over by the great *Tyee*, King Gold, and his retinue of Indians and miners, and a giant carnival midway located on "the large open tract where Denny Hill was recently graded away". A public information booth was set up under the comfort station roof in Pioneer Place and the old guard of transient workers and soap box prophets was elbowed back to the Skid Road proper.

The orators and their audiences moved, but the Potlatch failed to divert them otherwise. The grimy brick walls of the Skid Road continued to echo verbal blasts against the parasitic millionaires, and the red card of the I. W. W. was becoming the passport of the working stiff.

The I. W. W. anticipated the Potlatch celebration the following year by parading through town on a late spring afternoon of 1912 with the red flag of revolution flying beside the Stars and Stripes at the head of the marching column. Mayor Cotterill announced that, in his opinion, they had as much right to stage a parade as did the *Tilikums of Elttaes* or the G. A. R. Since there was no law against making speeches or holding parades, said Cotterill, interference by the police would not be law enforcement but just another form of the anarchy the "Wobblies" were advocating.

Neither the man on the street nor the *Times* would buy the Mayor's legal nicety, however. Spectators broke up the Wobbly parade in a fist-swinging riot for possession of the red flag, while Colonel Blethen trumpeted like a bull elephant in agony. Mayor Cotterill, the "Friend of the Red-Flag Anarchists" was encouraging the downfall of everything sacred, including Home, Motherhood, and the Ranier Club. The *Times,* the Colonel said, *"Is waging a single-handed fight for Old Glory, gladly standing on the firing line for the honor of the Flag and our country".*

The Colonel's direst predictions were, he felt, born out in February of 1913, when the *Times* building at Second and Union caught on fire. The fire department listed the cause as "unknown", but the Colonel had his suspicions. *"Our building was destroyed",* he wrote in a bylined editorial, *"but our flag flew through the fire unscorched. We don't know that the enemies of the flag and the country did this thing, but so fiendishly was the fire kindled that it has never seemed within the bounds of reason that it could have been commenced in any other way than at the hands of the Reds".*

The failure of the flames to bring down the flag meant a

lot to Colonel Blethen, whose patriotism wasn't assumed. The passing of Old Glory frequently brought tears to his eyes, and he made a ceremony of raising the *Times* flag every morning.

"*But our flag stayed up*", he continued proudly, "*They could destroy our building—they even might destroy the paper's heads—but the* Times *is an institution greater than all the men contained in it—a living thing that shall go on forever laboring in the cause of right and justice no matter what comes to individuals connected with it*".

Seattle was almost grown up, but one more good, unrestrained temper tantrum had to be gotten out of the city's system first. It reached its climax in the Potlatch Days of July, 1913.

Journalistically the dispute had crossed the party lines. The conservative *Post-Intelligencer* didn't like the Wobblies any better than Colonel Blethen did, but it was reluctant to agree with the *Times* in anything. Even the *P. I.* weather predictions varied from those of the genial Umbrella Man on the front page of the *Times*. The *P. I.* accordingly took a position which might be described as one of biased neutrality. The evening *Star*, which generally followed a path of least resistance, followed the *P. I.* line, while the daily *Union-Record,* performed its duty of speaking out for labor. Its editorials were echoed by the myriad labor weeklies and monthlies which seldom found their way above First Avenue. The more or less Democratic *Times* continued to lead the fight against anarchy and Seattle's more or less Democratic Mayor.

July, 1913, was hot and sultry, but the Third Potlatch opened with good-natured revelry. Boy Scouts led a mammoth children's parade which featured a life-sized Viking ship from Ballard Playground. The Pacific Fleet was in the harbor to add to the festivities and Seattle has had a special soft spot in its heart for the Navy ever since the U. S. S. *Decatur* saved the town from the Indians.

The Secretary of the Navy, Josephus Daniels, was in town, too. On the seventeenth he reviewed a military parade with sailors from the fleet, soldiers from the Puget Sound artillery forts and American flags in such profusion that Colonel Blethen was still misty-eyed when he went to the Rainier Club that evening for the banquet at which Daniels was to be the featured speaker.

The Secretary of the Navy delivered a stirring patriotic speech, a routine praising of freedom, the Constitution and the American way of life. It was the same speech he had made several times before in other cities, but without the blessings of radio and television the habitues of the Rainier Club had no way of knowing that.

It was probably as much a surprise to Daniels as it was to Mayor Cotterill, who had been at the banquet, when the *Times* reported the next day that the Secretary of the Navy had delivered a stinging personal rebuke to the Mayor of Seattle . . . *"Made it"*, the *Times* said, *"in the pallid presence"* of the Mayor, who *"sat green and sweaty under the Secretary's terrible blast"*.

The Mayor denied that he had been rendered either green or sweaty by the speech; that he had enjoyed it thoroughly and hadn't been aware that he was included in it. He was more disturbed by other glaring *Times* headlines in the same issue, which asserted that *"While Daniels Arouses Patriotism at Rainier Club"*, the red-flag anarchists of the Skid Road had attacked and brutally beaten American soldiers and sailors who had tried to take action against I. W. W. insults to the flag.

Mayor Cotterill launched an investigation while *Times* political reporters roamed the Skid Road interviewing "well known authorities" and "usually reliable sources". The police informed the Mayor that the riot had started when a sailor preempted the soap box of a lady orator named Annie Miller, a militant pacifist who was not connected with the I. W. W. When Mrs. Miller tried to reclaim her rostrum a sailor raised a threatening fist and was promptly knocked down by someone in the crowd. Passing artillerymen had rushed to the aid of the Navy and been thoroughly slapped around by embattled sympathizers of Annie Miller.

As far as the cops were concerned, it was just another of the street corner brawls with which they had been coping for a number of years. The Admiral of the visiting fleet reported that all his boys had made it back from shore-leave and that from the Navy's viewpoint there were no complaints to be made and no investigation required. He added that he thought "this year's Potlatch is far ahead of the former one I had the honor of witnessing and those in charge should be congratulated for the smooth way in which everything is going off".

The *Times,* however, was not to be diverted from its crusade. It made it clear that it expected red-blooded Americans to join with the boys in blue to revenge the insults to the flag and the lumps and bruises of Seattle's uniformed guests. A prominent National Guard officer who had resigned his commission at the outbreak of the Spanish-American War, but regained it in time to welcome the boys back, was quoted as advocating that the anarchists be run out of town without delay. A veterans' leader said that his boys would be down at Wobbly headquarters with everything "from bolos to head axes". It was further intimated that enlisted men of the Army and Navy would be on hand to "decisively answer any insult".

Mayor Cotterill was of the opinion that the *Times* was trying to make a volcano out of a molehill, but wasn't quite sure what to do about it. While he was thinking things over, thousands of Seattle citizens and Potlatch visitors were gingerly approaching the Skid Road. Mayor Cotterill didn't have 66,000 paid subscribers and Colonel Blethen did. All of them had been informed by the *Times* that big things were brewing on the Skid Road and they wanted to be in on them.

At some indeterminate point on the evening of July eighteenth, that good-humored Potlatch crowd turned into a mob. With uniformed soldiers and sailors much in evidence, it swept through the Skid Road to Wobbly headquarters. The red card holders were pushed aside by sheer weight of numbers and the hall was thoroughly smashed to pieces. I. W. W. literature was piled in the gutter and burned. Then, for good measure, the mob demolished a newsstand which was alleged to sell socialist newspapers, wrecked the Socialist Hall and finished the evening's festivities by tearing up an unoffending Gospel Mission.

The Mayor knew he had trouble on his hands. The police hadn't fired on the mob and the Skid Roaders hadn't been organized for real resistance, so there had been no bloodshed, except in the columns of the *Times,* which inferred that servicemen had been carried off to hospitals with anarchist knives sticking out of them like quills on porcupines. Cotterill knew that the coming weekend would bring an army of Wobbly working stiffs to town and that the next riot might turn the Potlatch-decorated streets into slaughter-pens.

The Mayor mobilized the police and fire departments, cancelling all leaves and taking personal charge of his forces. The *Times* observed that *"Anarchy, the grizzly hydra-headed monster which Seattle has been forced to nourish in its midst by a naturalized chief executive for eighteen months, was plucked from the city and wiped out in a blaze of patriotism last night".*

Cotterill had already ordered the city's saloons closed for the duration of Potlatch and had banned all street meetings. The *Times'* latest blast convinced him that these other safeguards would be ineffective unless he could silence Colonel Blethen and he could think of only one way of silencing that choleric publisher short of having him shot. The Mayor sent a detachment of police to the *Times* building with orders to prevent distribution of the paper within the city limits . . . unless all copy were submitted to him for approval before publication. The response of Colonel Blethen to this ultimatum can better be imagined than described. When he was finally able to speak clearly he reached for his much abused telephone. (Once, when he had been badly scooped by the *P. I.,* he is said to have torn that instrument from the wall and hurled it out the window in the direction of Erastus Brainerd's office.) This time he called Fulton and Kelleher, his attorneys.

Within a few hours the *Times'* legal talent had a restraining order from Judge Humphries, a highly conservative jurist who was more than moderately annoyed by the attempt of a Democratic Mayor to interfere with the normal profits of business, whether in newspapers or whiskey. For good measure the Colonel got an order requiring the Mayor to let the saloons reopen. The *Times* had an evening edition on the streets that night, but the saloons had been closed for some time and the Colonel had been too busy with legal problems to build up a really good head of steam. The city was sobering up.

The *Times* reached an all-time climax of indignation in its edition of July twentieth. The front page was printed entirely in red, white and blue. Big headlines across the top announced: *"Mayor Cotterill Names Himself King"*. Below that, the whole upper half of the page was given over to a huge, full-color reproduction of the Stars and Stripes. Down in the lower corner the kindly old Umbrella Man and his jaunty duck were shown leaving town for the weekend.

Most of the paper was given over to an account of the Mayor's effort to "throttle the freedom of the press". In the process it referred to him variously as *"this despised man"*, *"the advocate of anarchy and leader of the red-flag gang"*, *"this despoiler of the English language"*, *"this discredited, dishonest and loathed mayor of Seattle"*, and *"this froglike thing"*. The kindest thing the Colonel had to say about the Mayor was that *"apparently the man went insane"*.

Aside from its attack on Cotterill it was a fairly moderate edition, however, announcing firmly that there would be no more riots in Seattle. For the next month or so Colonel Blethen was so mad at Mayor Cotterill that there was little space left over for blasting the I. W. W. Potlatch Days ended in relative peace and quiet. The nine ships of the Pacific Fleet steamed across the bay to Bremerton and most of the Wobblies went back to the timber camps. Seattle had staged another noisy, sensational upheaval without loss of life.

But the scars remained and spread across the Northwest. The working stiffs were convinced that the Army and Navy had been called in to break up their "One Big Union". People who had homes and families and steady jobs had been led to view the Wobblies as bomb throwing monsters. The bitterness and suspicion grew into more violence and real bloodshed. A steamer-load of Wobblies from Seattle was met at the Everett city dock by a vigilante committee armed with rifles, and somebody pressed a trigger. Men slumped down and died on the steamer's deck and on the dock.

The feeling of the time is portrayed by the case of a wealthy mill-owner's son who was on the dock to see the excitement. He took a bullet through the lungs. He was wearing stagged pants and a logger's shirt, so the kindly doctor who came to attend him mistook him for a Wobbly and kicked him in the head.

The Wobblies were taken back to Seattle to be lodged in jail, charged with murder. Hi Gill, back in the mayor's office then, aroused new and hysterical threats of a recall when he went down to the jail to hand out pipe tobacco to the prisoners. Hi's corncob was almost a part of his diminutive anatomy by that time, and he could sympathize with a man who needed a smoke; besides, he made it clear, the "Everett Massacre" wouldn't have happened if the Everett authorities hadn't "acted like a bunch of imbeciles" and the vigilantes like "a gang of cowards".

The papers didn't agree with the Mayor. They were unanimous, all but the little *Union-Record,* in the opinion that Red-coddling mayors like Cotterill and Gill had caused the tragedy when they extended the rights of free speech and public assemblage to the Skid Road rabble.

Almost everyone agreed with the newspapers, but former prosecuting attorney George Vanderveer was an exception. In his younger days he had delighted in punching Wobbly orators off their soap boxes and he was still convinced that they were a bunch of wild-eyed fanatics, but he just couldn't help taking the side of the under dog; besides, anything he could do for them would be a sort of post-mortem blow to Colonel Blethen, who had died the year before. On one of the occasions when the Colonel had threatened to run Vanderveer out of town the fighting prosecutor had promised that he would be around to, as they say in the Army, "commit a nuisance" on the Colonel's grave. Defending the Everett Wobblies successfully would be a highly satisfactory substitute.

Vanderveer did defend them, ripping the prosecution's

case to shreds and freeing them in the face of overwhelming public hatred. Later, when sickening violence flared in Centralia, with legionaires shot in the streets and Wobblies obscenely mutilated and dragged through the streets behind speeding automobiles, Vanderveer defended the survivors in their murder trial. Some strange compulsion drove this man, acknowledged to be the greatest trial lawyer in the West, to take up the battle of despised men who had no money, no friends and little hope. It drove him from the security of a lucrative law practice to the edges of the Skid Road and to bankruptcy.

It was only after the Wobbly cause was dead and there were no more wild-eyed fanatics to defend that this remarkable man went back to the respectable pursuit of making money, an activity which, in a few years gave him shares in a score of profitable enterprises and ownership of the not so profitable Seattle Coast League ball club.

Vanderveer is gone now, along with most of the other leading actors on the stage of adolescent Seattle; Hi Gill and Colonel Blethen, Chief Wappenstein and Mark Matthews and the Wobblies who, whatever else they might have been, were men of courage who scorned the Communist doctrine of underground plotting and went down fighting in the open.

The *Star* and the *Union-Record* are only vague memories now, and the Pulitzer-winning *Times* has grown ever more sober and decorous than the *P. I.* Neither paper has taken a good roundhouse swing at the other for more years than anyone can remember. Perhaps the ghosts of Colonel Blethen and Erastus Brainerd turn as restlessly as that of Chief Seattle, for the two-fisted personal journalism of their era died with them.

Rolland Denny, who had come ashore from the *Exact* to a roofless cabin in the rain at Alki Point, died under the gathering clouds of a second World War. His lifetime had seen a city of half a million rise from the empty shores of Elliott Bay and he was the last link with its first beginnings.

The cocky, clanging cable cars are gone, and the jaunty little steamboats of the Mosquito Fleet, which used to sail from Colman Dock. There are no soap box orators left at

Pioneer Place and no one to listen to them if there were. Most of the loggers are home watching television, or maybe out driving with their families in two-toned automobiles.

Seattle has grown up and the really turbulent days are past. The city of 1915 was the beginning of New Seattle.

Some say the city didn't come of age until after the General Strike that followed World War I. Others point to the wartime shipyard foreman who, according to legend, was sealed up in the double bottom of a cargo ship by his rivet-crew who objected to his old fashioned ideas of discipline; or to the goon-squads of imported thugs who cracked heads and broke arms over curbstones in the labor troubles of the 1930's.

But these were brief and isolated acts of violence. The General Strike was really an example of the responsibility that comes with maturity. It failed because the working people who engineered it had developed social consciences of their own and were reluctant to cause real suffering to gain their ends.

The terror bred of the Potlatch Riots was the last symptom of regional infantilism—the refusal of one side to admit of a single grain of goodness or reason in the other. It was the same force that caused the Indian War and the Chinese Riots and the lynchings in front of Henry Yesler's house.

Seattle has grown up, and in the growing it has become more a part of America; less an arrogant young giant standing by itself on the rim of the last frontier. In the process it has sacrificed some of its individuality, but less than most cities. It still has a personality which is all its own—a rare thing in a standardized land.

You feel Seattle's individuality in many quarters; in the color and confusion of Pike Place Market, on the Marion Street Viaduct where the sea breeze brings the smell of salt and ships, in the quiet residential streets of city and suburbs, where the people seem to keep their houses brighter and their lawns greener than people who live anywhere else in the world.

Most of all you'll feel it when you take the time for an unhurried walk down Yesler Way from City Hall Park to

Pioneer Place. East and north of there, as it has been observed before, you're walking on real estate, but there you're walking through history.

To the right the Smith Tower still looms as the tallest building in the West and to the left the Skid Road is still a likely place to find trouble if you're looking for it. This was the little plot of ground that held the sawmill of Henry Yesler and Doc Maynard's shabby drugstore and the hotel of Mother Damnable. Here was fought the Battle of Seattle and the tall fir tree that hid Cornelius Hanford's Indian had grown where the Smith Tower stands. From here the horse cars jogged down to Pike Street and here the city took its stand against the Great Fire.[2]

Pioneer Place is one of the triangles that resulted from Doc Maynard's stubbornness in refusing to make his plat fit those of the other founding fathers and it has stubbornly refused to observe the passing of the years. The sleek automobiles and hissing trolley-coaches slip by it, but their passengers are insulated from it. The Place itself hasn't changed.

The fancy arcade of the comfort station, unused for years, still guards the south end of the triangle like an antiquated subway entrance. Men who are down on their luck still share the park benches with the strolling pigeons, gazing blankly at the blank windows of dingy buildings that were the first to rise from the ashes of the Fire. There are more empty snoos cans than cigarette butts amid the pigeon droppings of Pioneer Place; the scars from the spiked boots of angry loggers still mark the paving there, and you realize that frontier days are not really so long past after all.

At the northern apex of the triangle the bronze face of Chief Seattle is turned toward the hills that still stand to the north, mildly contemplating the city that took his name, just as he always did in life. Behind him stands the Totem Pole, its barbaric colors glowing bright in the grime of its surroundings.

The Totem Pole tells of history too, but not the history

---

[2] The Fire Sale signs are still up in this neighborhood, too.

of Seattle. Its story is the story of another race of men who lived on a rocky island to the north, preying on their gentler neighbors in a grim fight for survival. The figures of their Totem reflect their way of life.

If Seattle ever gets around to carving itself a personal Totem Pole the figures will be much different, for they will be telling the story of a city that has never known defeat and has never quite parted with its sense of humor or the sense of proportion that goes with it. Most of the figures on Seattle's Totem will be smiling . . . and quite a few of them will be remembering the best loved legends of all from our city's legendary past . . .

They'll be laughing.

The End

TOTEM TRANSLATIONS
FOR THOSE WHO LIKE TO CHECK THE ANSWERS

CHAPTER 1

Nervous pioneers, on a backdrop of the schooner *Exact's* hull, find the odors of cooking salmon too much for them, arrive sad and seasick at the unfinished log cabin on Alki Point, where skunks have eaten the food of David Denny whose aching jaws were tied up in a rag. It's no wonder the lady pioneers wept.

CHAPTER 2

Chief Seattle, known to white settlers as a man of peace, once rattled the gambling bones and used a British musket to end the career of an unsuccessful medicine man. His greatest military victory was achieved by felling a big fir tree across the Duwamish River to mow down attacking Muckleshoots in their canoes.

CHAPTER 3

Infant Rolland Denny survives on a diet of clam juice, while his elders sound Elliott Bay with Mary Denny's clothesline and Charles Terry's horseshoe. Ashore, the ladies had trouble with prying Indians, but soon learned methods of retaliation. Doc Maynard's fish-packing venture is an ill-smelling failure, but Henry Yesler's sawmill is a huge success . . . except for a group of bewildered legislators who warmed themselves at its boiler in the mistaken idea that they were aboard a steamboat.

CHAPTER 4

City fathers plat the city streets, but Doc Maynard's whiskey jug dampens their enthusiasm and leads to some confusion. Dexter Horton puts up a bold front at his new bank, while Chief Seattle annoys Governor Stevens on his round of treaty-making. The Battle of Seattle leads to violence, not all of it against the Indians, forcing settlers to rush to the blockhouse in the middle of their breakfasts. The last shot, fired years later, deposits banker Horton in a bramble patch.

CHAPTER 5

The calliope-equipped *Eliza Anderson* carries cows and mail from Puget Sound to British Columbia, but outrages Canadian law and order when the calliope player celebrates the Fourth of July with an impromptu concert in the pre-dawn hours. In later years even more excitement was caused when a

Colman Dock gangplank broke, depositing scores of would-be steamboat passengers in Elliott Bay.

CHAPTER 6

Doc Maynard remains Seattle's leading physician despite his whiskey bottle, his two wives, and such tricks as putting scraps of paper marked "18" in the shoes of youthful brides. Not so well beloved was tough Madam Damnable, with her apron full of rocks and her vicious dogs. But even she was tamed by a doughty tar from the U.S.S. *Decatur*.

CHAPTER 7

Happy males welcomed the arrival of the "Pennell Girls" to staff the town's first brothel, but Asa Mercer, pillar of the Territorial University brought respectability with his shipload of "Mercer Girls". Seattle continued to cavort happily with the painted ladies down on the sawdust, but expelled poor Mercer, whose pure damsels had cost more than the town could afford.

CHAPTER 8

The motto of Washington Territory's seal meant "by-and-by", but when it came to railroads, Seattle wasn't willing to wait. Judge Thomas Burke took personal command of a locomotive to win one railroad battle, and even the stubborn Northern Pacific gave in when embattled farmers planted potatoes on the right-of-way and tore up ties for fence posts.

CHAPTER 9

Lynch law took over briefly in Seattle, to be followed by more violence during the anti-Chinese riots. The judicial gavel was topped by the axes of door-smashing rioters, while dignified judges were horrified . . . and helpless.

CHAPTER 10

Streetcar horses give way to the strange and mysterious force of electricity, with Judge Burke's Ballard line straining the generative powers of the Burke Building to the utmost. In the end streetcars and cable cars alike are burned in the flames of progress, just as was the wooden business district of Old Seattle in the Great Fire of 1889. Feebly spurting fire engines were no match for the flames from an overturned glue pot in the town cabinet shop.

CHAPTER 11

The City Treasurer tried to make everybody happy in reform days . . . and ended up in jail, while box houses were closed and whiskey supplies cut off on the Lava Beds . . . until the arrival of a "Ton of Gold" on the Alaska liner *Portland* sparked the Gold Rush and brought crowds of well-healed treasure seekers to Seattle. Then a change was in the air and

John Considine came back to town, looking for good cellar locations south of Yesler Way.

CHAPTER 12

Honest Tom Humes "opens up the town" to celebrate the Alaska Gold Rush which brings lots of ready cash to town, of which John Considine and other Tenderloin operators get their share, with the cooperation of an obliging police department, but with tragic results when displaced Police Chief Meredith goes out gunning for Considine.

CHAPTER 13

The steep hills which have strangled Seattle's growth are washed away by hydraulic mining methods, after which people are no longer drowned on downtown streets, although the city's two major newspapers are unable to agree on the virtues of this operation. Colonel Blethen of the *Times*, feeling the regrade hoses syphoning tax dollars out of his purse, trades punches with Erastus Brainerd of the *P.I.*, while turning his big guns on City Engineer R. H. Thomson, whose head is in a cloud of more grand (and expensive) schemes for civic betterment. And all the time, rival cities look upon the much vaunted Seattle Spirit as a bulb-snatching wolf.

CHAPTER 14

Mayor Hi Gill is blasted out of office by the Rev. Dr. Mark Matthews and the Forces of Decency, after which Police Chief Wappenstein is found to be a man of two official faces and an ever receptive purse, with the result that he retires to the state prison at Walla Walla and Hi Gill "gets religion". The reelected Mayor smashed a lot of whiskey barrels, but couldn't prevent his sinful city being put "Off Limits" by the Army during World War I.

CHAPTER 15

Seattle steals itself a totem pole, which later is reclaimed by the Indians and finally fatally damaged by internal fire, while the Umbrella Man comes to town to shoot pin pool and make Seattle weather famous. Then, as now, football holds the popular attention, although Skid Road orators preach violence amid a flurry of red Wobbly cards, and the L. C. Smith typewriter empire spawns a Seattle skyscraper which is 42 stories high (if you count the basements).

CHAPTER 16

The Potlatch Bug, which typified Seattle's first big civic festivals, was the symbol for a lot of fun, but there were Potlatch Days that weren't so funny. When the "Red Flag of Anarchy" and a crusading newspaper publisher got into the act things took a violent turn, but any philosophical historian looking back on Seattle's past will inevitably come to the conclusion that there were more smiles than scowls in the story of our city.

THE BARBARY COAST

An Informal History
of the San Francisco Underworld

Herbert Asbury

For 70 years, the Barbary Coast was a haven for hoodlums and splendid happenings. Sydney Ducks, Chinese tongs, harlots and confidence men battled in the alleys, while Colonel Hayes defeated Bryant astride a black charger in Portsmouth Square, and glamourous madams opened the doors of the most luxurious establishments in the West.

Today it is part of the past—only this classic study remains to remind us of this turbulent and colorful chapter in San Francisco's history.

$1.65

A COMSTOCK EDITION

To order by mail, send price of book plus
25¢ per order for handling to Ballantine Cash
Sales, P.O. Box 505, Westminster, Maryland
21157. Please allow three weeks for delivery.

A TOUCH OF
OREGON

Ralph Friedman

This is the latest verse in a continuing love song to the state and history of Oregon. It sends you on a pilgrimage along rugged coasts, across desert and wheatfields, through orchards and up majestic mountains.

But more than that, it explores the dimensions of the people—men and women of a unique breed, whose characters have been given special expression by life in a magnificent state—whose destinies have been touched by Oregon.

$1.75

A COMSTOCK EDITION

To order by mail, send price of book plus 25¢ per order for handling to Ballantine Cash Sales, P.O. Box 505, Westminster, Maryland 21157. Please allow three weeks for delivery.